ON LAW AND IDEOLOGY

LANGUAGE, DISCOURSE, SOCIETY

Editors: Stephen Heath and Colin MacCabe

Working from recent advances in linguistics, semiotics, psycho-analysis and theory of ideology, the Language, Discourse, Society series is committed to forwarding an adequate account of the effective reality of meaning, sign, subject in the relations of signifying practices and social formations. That such an account must have implications and repercussions for the current terms of cultural and political understanding will be the constant edge of the series.

ON LAW AND IDEOLOGY

Paul Hirst

First published 1979 by
THE MACMILLAN PRESS LTD
London and Basingstoke
Associated companies in Delhi
Dublin Hong Kong Johannesburg Lagos
Melbourne New York Singapore Tokyo

Printed in Great Britain by
Billing & Sons Limited
Guildford, London and Worcester

British Library Cataloguing in Publication Data

Hirst, Paul
   On law and ideology. – (Language, discourse, society)
   1. Ideology
   I. Title   II. Series
   145   B823.3

   ISBN 0-333-25949-1
   ISBN 0-333-25950-5 Pbk

Contents

Acknowledgements

The author is grateful to *Economy and Society*, who gave permission to republish Chapter 3 which first appeared in Vol. 5, No. 4, 1976 and to Cambridge University Communist Party for making available the material which now forms Chapter 2.

He would also like to thank Barry Hindess for his help and critical comments.

1 On Ideology

Ideology has developed a significance and centrality in Marxist theory in the last decade which it had never possessed before. This change represents an attempt to come to terms with pressing political problems and struggles in modern capitalism. The Women's Movement, the struggles around the character and content of education, movements among Blacks and anti-racist struggles, questions of welfare state practices, the political role and effects of the mass media, and so on, have forced Marxists to recognise a complex field of social relations inadequately comprehended by the classic Marxist theories of the economy and politics. Louis Althusser's work is the primary means by which these problems, inadequately signalled under the notion of 'ideology', have been thought through in this country and in France. The three essays on ideology published here are different stages of my attempt to come to terms with and to criticise Althusser's work. This criticism is no mere dismissal; it attempts to take up and extend certain of Althusser's innovations in relation to Marxist theory. These innovations made possible a new kind of attention to certain political questions, and yet at the same time his concept of the 'ideological instance' closed-off an adequate theoretical response to those questions, restoring the theoretical continuity with classical Marxism which they had disturbed. It is this continuity that I began to challenge. Althusser's incorporation of this field of institutions, practices, discourses and struggles into his concept of social totality as the 'ideological instance' set serious limits on the forms of politics which could be considered appropriate within this field.

My criticism of Althusser has proved unacceptable to many Marxists because it has dismembered the prevailing general theory of the 'ideological' and makes no attempt to replace it with another. They see this criticism as merely negative. And so it would be if the only possible objective of theoretical work in this area was to unify the social relations in question in a general concept and locate them as an element in a social totality, an element which both serves to reproduce it as a totality and which in turn is subject to the logic of its reproduction. But it is precisely this objective that I am attacking.[1] Except as part of a totality, an entity governed by a principle of unity and necessary limits, these relations exhibit no *necessary* homogeneity. This means they cannot be represented in a general concept of their character and effects. It is not only questions of theoretical adequacy that lead me to challenge this objective. The consequences of a theory like Althusser's for the conception of the politics appropriate to this area of social relations are the main reasons for my opposition to this type of work. Clearly, the alternative I have offered cannot produce the same type of theoretical results. In rejecting a general theory of the 'ideological instance', insisting on the heterogeneity of 'ideological' social relations and their effects, I have tried to indicate the space for specific theorisations and questionings of institutions, practices and discourses in this area. The nature of this work cannot be legislated for in advance of its products, nor can it have an easy and unambiguous relation to Marxist theory.

There can be no doubt that the main effect of my criticisms is to challenge the pretensions of previous Marxisms, to radically limit the claims and competencies of Marxist discourses in relation to what are called 'ideological' social relations. Challenging the Marxist notion of totality means challenging Marxism's claims to competence as a general science of social relations. It means being prepared to accept that in questions of sexuality, family forms, methods of training and social control, and so on, conventional Marxism may have little that is positive to say and the classic prescriptions of socialist ideology may be at best irrelevant. This preparedness is essential if the socialist movement is to be able to ally itself with, to learn from, to draw strength from and to unify in practice a whole complex of movements, practices and struggles. In a sense Marxists and others have been coming to terms in their practice with this radical limitation for some time. Just as many people concerned in struggle in a particular area, such as, for example, welfare policy, have turned to Marxism and to socialism to gain a wider comprehension and ideological basis, so Marxists are increasingly being forced to take hitherto 'alien' discourses like psychoanalysis or the work of Foucault and his collaborators seriously for want of any adequate means within Marxism to come to terms with the problems they face.

This radical limitation of the claims and competencies of Marxist theories is part of a much wider challenge to previous conceptions of the relation of theory and practice. Barry Hindess and I have argued in *Mode of Production and Social Formulation* (*MPSF*) that Marxism is not a 'science' but a 'political theory', a medium of political calculation. That is, it is one of the means by which political situations of action are constructed and definite actions in relation to those situations determined. A 'political theory' serves calculation in two ways: it provides criteria of appropriateness of political actions (objectives, principles, 'ideology') and it provides discursive means for characterising the situation of action. The means employed in political calculation are not confined to political theory. The means of calculation are conditioned by and involve political apparatuses, practices and struggles and their effects. Theory has no necessary privilege in relation to this complex of means, it is in no sense necessarily primary in the construction of situations of action. Such modes of calculation have conditions of their operation in and are therefore limited by the practices for which they calculate. They are also, through these practices and their effects, conditioned and limited by the situations which they construct in calculation.

Discourses about politics, 'political theories', have a crucial organising and directing role in certain forms of politics. Marxism postulates such a role for discourse, claiming itself to be the 'unity of theory and practice'. This unity follows from the application to Marxist practice itself of its theory of social knowledge, historical materialism. Social being determines social consciousness, but the adequate apprehension of social being ('science') demands a specific form of social consciousness (Marxism). Marxism is both product of and a scientific guide to the situation of action; it thus makes possible the transformation of social reality because its practice conforms to the nature of that reality. This double connection, central to the claims of classical Marxism, must be challenged. Marxism links its theory of social causality and its theory of knowledge. Its conception of the relation between calculation and the situation of action is an epistemological one. Calculation appropriates the situation as object of knowledge, and that situation – as social being – ultimately determines that process (social causality assures the knowledge-being relation). Political calculation is knowledge of an object. In *MPSF* we argued that calculation *constructs* the situation of action, that that situation always exists to political practice in the form of a construct. Calculation cannot appropriate the situation of action as if it were an object of knowledge.[2] Among our general criticisms of epistemological discourse we argued that, in positing a necessary and general knowledge-being relation, epistemologies are forced to constitute being as a class of objects with attributes appropriate to the knowledge process by which it is corresponded to or appropriated. A necessary form of knowledge relation requires a reality appropriate to that relation. Marxism conceives social being to be a totality, its phenomena forming a unity of effects. Social being is therefore capable of representation as totality, of appropriation as a singular 'reality'.

Once we step outside of epistemological discourse then we must abandon the concept of 'knowledge'; with it we abandon the concepts of a unitary knowing subject and 'object' of knowledge, the latter a realm of being with general attributes assimilated or appropriated by the subject. The consequences of our critique of epistemology are reinforced by our challenge to the Marxist conception of social relations as forming a totality. It follows, if we do not conceive social relations as subject to a hierarchy of necessary determinations and articulations, that political situations and practices in a particular country or conjuncture can differ radically. There is no single point of reference for all practices. Political situations of action will differ with the types of arenas involved and the practices engaged in, with the contending forces and issues. It does not follow from this that we must therefore consider the political situations as the mere products of the outlooks and 'wills' of their participants. These situations and the nature of the participants themselves depend on definite conditions, but these conditions do not form a totality. Practices encounter obstacles and opposed forces which differ from their calculative constructions, practices do not determine their own conditions of existence. But these obstacles and forces have no necessary general attributes, they do not form a unitary 'reality' which confronts all practices. These obstacles and forces are assessed by the agents of practice in terms of definite forms of calculative construction; calculation is the continued adjustment of constructions to the conditions of practice.

It is an error to differentiate calculation and the situations it constructs in the same way as knowledge and its object. The situation is itself composed of anticipated states of affairs and the intersection of political practices. But calculative discourse does not exhaust political practice, nor is political practice itself unconditional. The construction of situations of action refers to conditions with effects. But the effectivity of the situations calculated on the practice of calculation is not that of a reality, they have no single origin and no necessary pattern of effects. The situations calculated in no sense add up to a single 'political reality'. They are differentiated not least by the types of political practice adopted. This radically effects the conditions of construction. These practices are not merely given in conditions anterior to them, ideology and the construction of strategies play an important part in the political mode adopted. I will attempt to illustrate this non-unity of the situations of calculation. Take a particular Marxist party, say a western European communist party: at any given time it may be involved in a number of practices, intra-party struggles over ideology and programme, parliamentary campaigns, competition with other groups to lead, annex or even stifle social struggles and mass movements; each of these offers distinct conditions for applying criteria of what should be done and the characterisation of the situation for that type of action. These diverse calculations of situations do not sum up to form a 'reality'. What they do when they are brought together is to generate conflicts as to the priority of forms of struggle and the criteria for constructing a hierarchy of such forms. This extends the circle of calculations and conflicts over criteria but does not close it. Marxism is not a 'science' (equally it is not a 'non-science', science-ideology is an epistemological distinction), it has no privileged knowledge (independent of political practice) of the nature and movement of social relations or of the adequacy of political actor's constructions of those relations.

The paradox is that as a 'political theory' Marxism has derived much of its power and appeal from the claim to be a science, to be able to determine the nature and development of social relations and to act according to the objective dictates of that knowledge. It has thereby solved problems of the criteria of appropriateness of action and the means for characterising the situation of action in one and the same operation, knowledge. In its claim to be a science it has been able to eschew questions about the objectives of its practice and the content of its political programme. Both are drawn from the necessities of social development and the realities of the class struggle. In terms of this claim Marxism has staked the whole content of its ideology on the postulated necessity of certain states of affairs. This claim has radically weakened its capacity to respond to conditions of struggle other than those outlined in the texts almost everyone agrees to be simplistic or problematic and yet is forced to adhere to, Marx's '1859 Preface' or Lenin's *State and Revolution*. The reason for this is that Marxism's criteria of appropriateness are contained in constructions of certain anticipated states of affairs. Thus the key Leninist criterion for evaluating political practices in relation to the state, the thesis of its 'withering away', is posulated as a necessary process rather than as an objective to be pursued in struggle. If 'withering' were not thought of as an objective necessity of the process of transition to communism then the problems of its nature as an objective of practice and criterion of evaluation might lead to some critical reformulation of socialist ideology. 'Withering' has come to appear a hollow notion as a result of our experience of socialist regimes; the general effect of that experience is to discredit Marxism. The category is either abandoned, rejected by 'democratic socialists' as a cynical claim made to facilitate Marxist rule, or made a matter of faith on the assumption that things will work out differently in more favourable conditions. As a result political ideology withers into something to forget, or dogma. Non-authoritarian social relations cease to be thought through as a political objective and a guide to political practice.

The content of Marxist political theory, 'ideology' (in the sense of a system of political ideas), cannot be rethought or reconstructed to meet new conditions of calculation and practice without challenging the claims of science, and without questioning one of Marxism's most compelling claims *as a political ideology*. Marxism is threatened by any radical accommodation to new conditions of calculation precisely because it has claimed to have established the *possible* conditions and determined at the most general level the necessary states of affairs. Given the concept of social totality and its movement Marxism has abolished for itself the space to mutate in relation to new political circumstances, if these circumstances are not compatible with its postulation of the effects of capitalism as totality then they threaten its existence by threatening its claim to truth. To the extent that politics has diverged from Marxism's constructions, notably the sustained development of capitalist economies and the continued survival of parliamentary democratic regimes with mass support in certain key capitalist countries, it has been disarmed in relation to those situations. The modes of accommodation made by Marxists are revealing. The withdrawal into the prediction of crises and revolutions to come, a withdrawal from current politics, or the acceptance, *without theoretical reconstruction*, of these political conditions, adaptation by making concessions in ideology, have been the parallel responses. Marxism has frozen into 'anti-revisionism' or melted into a political 'realism' which fails to consider what it means to fight for socialism under conditions set by parliamentary democracy. Scientism has crippled our capacity to think through and adapt our ideology to different political conditions. Our challenge to pretensions, and our insistence upon limits, are not conducted in the interests of reducing Marxism. Marxism in western Europe, despite its immense intellectual popularity, has reduced itself *as political theory* to virtual political irrelevance. The *political* irrelevance of an orthodoxy waiting for its postulated future. The irrelevance to politics of a Marxism which, mutilated by accommodation to conventional suppositions of the conditions of parliamentary success, represents the nominal ideology of the main European communist parties.

These remarks are not directed against 'political theory' or 'ideology'. To deny theory the role of 'knowledge', to challenge the pretensions to 'science', is not to deny the crucial organising and directing role that political discourse can and must have in socialist political practice. Socialism is nothing if it is not a political theory: a discourse which directs politics toward the construction of definite forms of social relations and in definite ways, a discourse which can construct and evaluate political situations (relative to definite objectives). Marxism has been the dominant form of socialist ideology. Its immense popularity is because it has formulated the objectives and content of socialist ideology. It prevailed in and took its character from opposition to the rationalism and moralism of Utopian socialism, and necessarily so. Socialist ideology has in consequence been carried by Marxist theory, entangled with the scientific pretensions and limits of that theory. Marxism has in consequence been inescapable *as theory*, unsupplantable because of what it carried and supported. Political practice cannot dispense without calculation, and calculation, beyond the politics of preservation of established and opportunist cliques, demands criteria of appropriateness: in a word, 'ideology'. For this reason socialists have held on to Marxism despite its defects. Modern socialism requires a revolutionary transformation in its political theory and the mode of constituting and presenting its political objectives. Theory that is limited neither by scientism, which fuses political objectives with certain necessary states of affairs, nor by the rationalism of moralism which reduces those objectives to 'goals'. Only the broadest recognition and discussion of the need for change and of its content can achieve this; recognising the limits of classical Marxism is merely a start. Ideology can only be reconstituted on a mass basis, learning from failures and innovations in forms of socialist struggle, attempting to adapt these forms to current political conditions, and from struggles, outside the ideological orbit of conventional Marxism, which have the objective of constructing co-operative, non-authoritarian social relations. The development of a 'political theory' broad enough to contain these elements is a crucial condition for uniting and multiplying these various struggles. A unity which is crucial to the restoration of the political strength and content of modern socialism. This implies no rejection of what Marxist theory has sought to attain, rather it is the reconstruction of the means of presenting those objectives and the means of constructing political situations of action.

Theories of 'ideology' such as have hitherto prevailed in Marxism can make no contribution to this reconstruction and development of socialist political ideology. The position presented in *MPSF* and in my essays radically extends the destruction of the pretensions of Marxist theories of ideology which Althusser began. It extends criticism to the foundations of those theories in theories of knowledge. It challenges the claims of those theories to scientificity and to 'knowledge', including Althusser's own. It is important to remember that Althusser's questioning of what had passed for 'obvious' in post-war Marxist theory, the claims of empiricism, humanism and historicism, made this much more radical challenge to and reconstruction of Marxist theory possible. In denying ideology was 'false consciousness' Althusser broke with the classic claim within Marxism to be able to differentiate between *forms of social consciousness* as true or false representations of social reality. He challenged the sociologisation of political ideology. Marxism could no longer be considered as it so often has been within 'orthodox' Marxism as basically the world outlook of a class raised to the level of science. But he did so by making Marxist *science*, historical materialism, a practice with a decisive atonomy from the social formation. In this way knowledge of social relations could direct mass practices based on an *imaginary lived relation* to those relations. Marxism appropriated the real in the realm of abstraction and returned to the real the knowledges thus gained by guiding the practice of politics. Politics required theoretical practice because social consciousness could never attain to knowledge of the social formation. Strategy was the political extension of the knowledges produced by theory. Althusser defined theoretical practice by means of a construction of Marx's conception of method in *Capital* and at the same time severed Marxism's connection with all sociologistic conceptions of knowledge as the reflection in consciousness of social being; something Marx did not do (as the theory of 'fetishism' stands witness).

Althusser has been in retreat from the implications and impossible pretensions of this position ever since the 'Foreword' to the Italian edition of *Reading Capital*. But he has never theoretically come to terms with them. *Theoretical Practice* took these implications as a necessary and valuable part of the theory and tried to develop on this basis the theoretical conditions for a political strategy appropriate to modern Britain. It failed, as it necessarily must have. Althusser's theory, for all its challenge to certain elements of orthodox Marxism, served as the philosophical underpinning for a traditional Marxist-Leninist conception of politics. But this failure made starkly obvious the problems of classical Marxism's claims to be a political knowledge. Both the conception of ideology as socially conditioned consciousness and as the imaginary representation of the structure to its agents involve the conception of a knowledge adequate to social relations: in the first case, the social consciousness of the class which represents the revolutionary nature of reality, and in the second, historical materialism, a practice without a subject, which appropriates the concrete in thought. Theories of ideology in Marxism have always been the realisation in social relations of theories of knowledge. The concept of ideology as part of an epistemological discourse has always involved the distinction of true and false (ideological) knowledges of reality. Althusser tried to break with this sociologisation of epistemological discourse, the attributing of truth to certain forms of social consciousness, but only by withdrawing questions of the adequacy of knowledge from the consciousness of social agents.

It is in this context that our insistence that Marxism as a political theory is neither *independent* of the situations which it calculates (these situations condition calculation in and through political practice) nor a *representation* of those conditions must be understood. The notion of a relation of 'knowledge' is challenged in this insistence, but not in the interests of scepticism (a position with vested interests in the continuation of the effects of epistemological discourse). The sociologisation of epistemological categories has rendered questions of the sources and content of socialist ideology unproductive; it has reduced them to what can be permitted in terms of answers based on class experience and the necessary effects of social relations. Althusser returns to this kind of sociologism in his paper on ideological state apparatuses (ISAs), as I have shown in Chapter 3, postulating a given 'ruling-class ideology'. Breaking the notions of the *autonomy* of theoretical knowledge and the *representational* nature of socially conditioned experience can actually help us to approach questions of political 'ideology' and calculation in a new and more constructive way. We can begin to investigate the conditions and limits of forms of political calculation. This investigation can aid political practice in sensitising it both to the role of calculation and to the effects of the conditions of calculation upon its means and its constructions. But this investigation can never itself step outside of the conditions of calculation. It can be no master knowledge of how to know, but the partial and problematic construction of the limits of political calculation. There can be no equivalent of the epistemological distinction between ideology and science. The effect of the absence of this criterion need not be a reckless disregard for analysis or the content of political claims. Nietzsche long ago showed that the effect of the decomposition of absolutes (or rather the fictional substitutes for them, for such there cannot be) is not nihilism. The recognition that everything is permissible was for him the foundation of a new sort of morality. Accepting the limits of political calculation and the absence of any necessary foundation for socialist ideology means that we must devote more care to assessing the conditions of and means of analysis, and to establishing what it is socialists make claim to and why it is so.

Our critique of the Althusserian theory of the social totality and of ideology involves the deconstruction of the field of 'ideological' social relations. This deconstruction has positive consequences in that it states certain of the terms on which socialists engage in political practice in this non-unitary area. What is insisted on in the criticism is the complexity and non-homogeneity of these social relations. In terms of the position advanced here, there can be no equivalent unifying concept to ISAs. The pertinence of the notion of 'ideology' to considering those relations is denied because the grip of a certain concept of totality over them is rejected: 'ideology' in its classical Marxist sense *means* categories which represent and organise the social actions of subjects in a certain necessary way, but which, in order to function in this way within social relations, must not constitute an adequate knowledge of those relations. Althusser's concept of 'ideology' retains these problems of functionality and misre-cognition. However much he attacks the notion of the 'falsity' of ideology, because he retains the distinction between ideology and science (even in the paper on *ISAs*) he must retain its equivalent (the 'misrecognition' effect of the 'imaginary relation'). Denying the epistemological problem of the validity of knowledge in terms of correspondence or non-correspondence to a 'real' object and the concept of totality as unity of being leaves no place for the theoretical problem of 'ideology'. A general theory of ideology has particular theoretical conditions of existence and is not an inevitability.

This positive reorientation in theory toward the heterogeneity of these relations parallels attempts in political practice to get beyond the workerism and essentialism of existing Marxist and socialist theories. In particular we are coming to and are being forced to realise that many important struggles cannot be aligned in terms of capitalism and anti-capitalism. Political issues and forces with a specificity which challenges this categorisation of alternatives force us to change our practice and our claims. Two contemporary examples should be sufficient here. The broadly based anti-racialist movement increasingly treats racism as a specific issue to be fought and won with all the allies and forces possible. The Women's Movement rightly refuses to be an auxiliary in the anti-capitalist struggle, its potential for generating far-reaching political and social change would be restricted if it were to do so. The Marxist *theoretical* response to movements such as these has been dismal (which is not to say non-Marxist responses are any better). Theories of racism as a product of imperialism and as ruling-class ideology, or of modern family forms as necessary to capitalist reproduction, attempt to place these questions within the confines of conventional socialist analysis, to subordinate them to a causality governed by the economic. As phenomena of capitalism they can be placed under the hegemony of socialist struggle. The problem is that as questions of political practice they obstinately refuse to resolve themselves in that way.

Althusser's central theoretical advance was to treat 'ideology' *as social relations*, to displace the notions of 'ideas' and 'consciousness' which had hitherto reduced ideology to a *representation in thought of social relations*. Althusser's central theoretical failure to break with classical Marxism was, paradoxically, an innovation within it: the theory of the 'ideological instance' as composed of 'ideological state apparatuses'. His advance was a massive one and he must be given due credit for it. The critique of ideology as 'consciousness' or 'ideas' effectively challenged the rationalism of conventional economistic positions. 'False consciousness' in the exploited class, a happy excuse for all sorts of political difficulties, such as racism, could always be posited as being overcome by some appropriate mixture of revolutionary propaganda and the evolution of the material conditions of class experience, such as an economic crisis. Ideology as a representation in consciousness of social relations removed its specificity/effectivity, it could always be displaced by the movement of social relations themselves. Ideology conceived as the effects of definite institutions and practices, as a form of organising and conducting social relations which cannot be dispensed with, could not be dealt with by classical economism. Its transformation could only be possible on the basis of specific practices directed at countering its effects. This conception appealed to socialists struggling in education, in or around social welfare institutions, against family forms and modes of subordination of women, etc., precisely because it freed them from the constraints of a certain form of economism. The object of their struggles ceased to be merely a *consciousness* of reality or the secondary effects of the primary economic contradiction. This is the main and progressive basis of Althusser's immense popularity. His work in this area was accepted by people hitherto ignorant of or hostile to the positions advanced in *For Marx* and *Reading Capital* a few years before.

Althusser also provided a theory of the location of these struggles in ISAs. This unified and attached a revolutionary strategic significance to those struggles, another major reason for his immense popularity. The ISAs were a means of reproducing capitalist relations of production, securing the conditions of existence of the capitalist mode of production by constituting subjects with attributes appropriate to its division of labour. The notion of reproduction thus explained the necessarily *capitalist* character of these social relations and that this character was necessary to the existence of capitalism as a totality; thus it posed class struggle at the level of the ideological instance as *revolutionary*. This has been a powerful legitimation against economism. It is also the source of the main political limitations in this theoretical position. It is wide open to ultra-leftism and excludes certain political practices which may enable socialists to make headway in European capitalist countries. ISAs are *state* apparatuses and unified by the ideology of the ruling class. Class struggle within and against them is possible but as such these apparatuses are confined within necessarily capitalist limits. In challenging the concept of totality which sustains Althusser's position we are also challenging its implications for the conception of politics. Our criticism challenges the basis for his characterisation of ISAs as *state* apparatuses and as forming a unity, a unity given in the ideology of the ruling class. The field of ISAs as the components of a unitary 'ideological instance' serving to reproduce capitalist relations of production is thus decomposed.

This decomposition has positive theoretical-political consequences. It follows from the criticism that all the institutions called ISAs (school, family, media, etc.) are not *necessarily* capitalist in character and effects. Nor are they 'state' apparatuses, dominated by ruling-class ideology. Whether constitutionally part of the state or not, they can be reformed and changed through state action, institutional initiatives and mass practice. The effect of such reforms and changes on wider social relations is not given and could be very radical indeed. Likewise particular institutions can possibly be transformed without radical change in other social relations as a concomitant or precondition. In the ISAs thesis legislative reform and state action to change institutions can only be within capitalist limits, apparatuses are merely differentiated parts of the state system subject to the necessities of reproduction. Reforms will merely be within the terms of and in order to serve that primary function. The ISAs thesis sharpens the reform/revolution dilemma by extending it to virtually all social relations.

Revolution or reform is a dilemma produced by essentialist theories of social relations. An index of Althusser's essentialisation of social relations is the identification (criticised in Chapter 3) of *occupational structure* and *social division of labour*. Radical changes in the composition of tasks, work skills and the organisation of work are possible within relations operating through wage labour and commodity forms. Struggles for equality for women, for workers' participation in management, the creation of workers' co-operatives all offer radical prospects for changing the composition of the work-force and the position of workers within enterprises. These changes threaten oppositions considered essential to capitalism by many Marxists such as the division of mental and manual labour: 'opening the books', for example, would provide vital information and means of control to workers' representatives and trade unionists, but it only does so on condition that they and their organisations acquire competence in accountancy. This process is already under way as a result of changes in disclosure provisions. To be effective, workers' participation in decision making (whether as part of legislation or an agreement forced on the enterprise by advanced trade union struggle) involves the acquisition of managerial skills and the formulation of policies for direction of the enterprise by a substantial number of employees. Changes of this kind can clearly react upon workers' attitudes to education and upon educational provision and make for changes in its character. Thus the clear implication of such a campaign for supervision and control of enterprises by the Labour movement would be a change in further education provision by the state, in trades unions, WEA and other sources. Women's struggle for equality, workers' demands for participation, producers' co-operatives, these struggles and forms are by no means fully developed; their full effects and implications lie in the future and are conditional on political practice. The Marxist left in this country has so far been hostile (with the exception of equality for women) because it has seen such struggles as reformist. (It should be noted that the essay on Law included in this volume examines the sources of this hostility and argues for a new approach to questions of company law and organisation.) Althusser's theory ultimately reinforces this opposition. Whilst workers' participation in no sense solves all problems of the 'managerial' administration of enterprises, and it is certainly true that decisions at enterprise level are not sufficient to transform the economic relations in which enterprises operate, this is to miss the point. What these examples show is that capitalist economies can continue to exist with very different occupational structures and practices of enterprise management than those hitherto supposed necessary by Marxists. Althusser sets the ISAs to guard and secure the conditions of capitalist production, but they are like blind bulldogs at the door of an empty fortress. The conditions of capitalist production are far more complex and flexible. ISAs which did constitute a labour force conditioned as Althusser supposes would require social relations of production as limited as their (ideological) conditions of existence. Wage labour and the production of commodities by enterprises for profit are compatible with a wide range of educational systems, management and occupational structures, family forms, etc. Our politics has to be capable of taking account of this.

By sharpening the refom/revolution dilemma and extending it to a broad and complex area of social relations the tendency of Althusser's position is to disarm the left. ISAs serve to reproduce capitalist relations and can only be opposed by revolutionary class struggle. In western Europe we face a protracted struggle under political conditions set by parliamentary democracy. Socialist parties and groups will need to use all possible sources of change and locations of struggle, not least because their prospects of forming effective administrations committed to socialist construction are limited in the foreseeable future. Reforms are not reformist if they create new grounds for struggle and new sources of strength. Because its effect is to minimise the possible forms of change within capitalist and commodity relations Althusser's position reinforces traditional conceptions of revolutionary socialist struggle and is an obstacle to innovations in political practice on the left. The left badly needs such innovations, forms of politics other than the competition for parliamentary majorities. These forms are vital because they offer the prospect of a mass base on which such a parliamentary majority could be built. The left needs to outflank its enemies, moving into areas and forms of struggle where the opposition is relatively unprepared and weak. The complex, inadequately denoted by the notion of 'ideological social relations', presents the primary example of such an opportunity. To seize it, changes in Marxist and socialist theory, ideology and conceptions of political struggle are necessary.

NOTES

1 The tendency to suppose that social relations must be conceived as a totality with a necessary structure, composed of certain 'instances' in definite relationships, is evidenced by Stuart Hall's remarks about the essay which now forms Chapter 3 (*Ideology and Consciousness*, 3, 120). Hall contends that the logic of my position is the 'necessary non-correspondence' of the instances of the totality. In that essay I argue that political forces and issues cannot be interpreted in terms of some postulate of their necessity of correspondence with the given 'interests' of classes of economic agents. What Hall does is to read this challenge to class essentialism, the insistence that there are no given class 'interests' against which politics can be measured, as a doctrine about the relation of *instances* in the totality. The notion of a 'non-correspondence' of instances in this sense is impossible and absurd, to think of 'instances' is to conceive their articulation into a totality. But what I and my co-authors are arguing for is the rejection of the concept of totality itself, and, therefore, the rejection of the problems of the relations of the political, economic, and other 'instances' in terms of heirarchy of causal effectivity, relative autonomy, etc. In our position political, economic and other social relations are not unified into 'instances', that is, definite sectors of the totality governed by their place in the whole and subject to its limits. Hall is adopting a practice analagous to those who charge us with arguing for the 'autonomy of the political'. Autonomy from what? This charge assumes that we retain the instances as entities but disentangle their relations, in effect promoting each to the status of an autonomous entity. How then is it possible to retain the concept of totality and how can those autonomous entities exist? The absurdity is not of our making, it results from the persistence of reading in terms of a certain social topography. Clearly, we do not think that political forces, apparatuses and issues are unconditional. What we *are* arguing is that those conditions cannot be specified in a general concept, as stemming, say, from the necessities and effects of the capitalist mode of production. This imposes on the instance thus conditioned a necessary general form, limits, and range of effects. Such a position is challenged in Marx's *Capital and Capitalism Today*, primarily because of its consequences for political analysis. To those who argue that the result is a 'Weberian' or 'neo-Kantian' pluralism we answer that in the first volume (Chapter 4, especially pp. 128–32) the field of contest of monism and pluralism is general doctrines of historical causality. It is precisely this field which we reject. General doctrines of historical causality require the privilege of their chosen categories of causation to be grounded in some way, secured against 'chance' and rival causal privileges. Thus Marxism does this by incorporating all social relations within a totality governed by the economic, and Hegelianism ultimately refers historical 'causation' to the internal development of a unitary and self-subsistent spirit. There is no necessity for the analysis of social relations to be predicated upon patterns of historical evolution, whether of the 'development of the forces of production', or Weber's 'rationalisation'. General doctrines of causality serve as the supports of these patterns but are not otherwise necessary to the analysis of specific forms of conditionality and connection between social relations. These

patterns are an incubus whose parasitic grip has long enslaved and enfeebled Marxism as a political theory.

2 Gregor McLennan (*Economy and Society* vol. vii no. 2) argues that the position of *MPSF* on calculation and epistemology is ambivalent and inconsistent: either we maintain a consistent relativism, insisting that the calculated exists only as and in discourse, or if we reject this consistent but sterile position, we are forced to recognise a non-discursive object of calculation, in effect to accept a 'reality' to which discourse refers and, therefore, the pertinence of epistemological categories. What McLennan does is to construct for us an option *within epistemological discourse*. Despite its sophistication the criticism refuses to come to terms with our criticism of epistemology as constructing a general relation between the categories of knowledge (discourse) and being (the object of knowledge). He distinguishes between two distinct realms, discourse and non-discourse, and thereby in effect restores the structure of the knowledge-being relation (and the options within it). Our objective was to *dissolve* this distinction. Knowledge and being are differentiated as distinct classes of categories and given general attributes as elements of a discourse which has as its object the posing of the possibility of a relation of *correspondence* between these two terms. We see no reason to retain this differentiation of categories in the absence of this problem. What is subject to calculation in our position is certainly not purely discursive. But what is calculated has *no necessary attributes*. The situations constructed in different calculations have no necessary and common reference point. To suppose this would be to ascribe common properties to the referents different discourses constitute and to suppose the parallel and autonomous existence of those referents to discourse (to restore 'being'). Further, the situations calculated and the referents' discourses speak of do not *exclude* calculations or discourses. Calculative discourses have no common 'referent' (distinct from discourse): political situations differ radically between forms of political practice and condition the calculations engaged in differently.

In *MPSF* we argue that there is no single 'situation' external to calculations and yet which is capable of being represented in such a way that it serves as the measure of those calculations made of it. Such a 'situation' presupposes political practices have a common referent and a common location. Such a 'situation' would be both *independent of calculative practice* (outside of and parallel to calculative discourse), and yet *capable of being represented*, capable of being intelligible as itself in relation to the calculative constructions made of it. This auto-intelligibility of the 'real', its capacity to be counterposed to the claims of knowledge of it, is the locus of a certain form of epistemological privilege: the source of this intelligibility is a *non-discursive representation of the real*, the source of the categories of 'experience', 'consciousness' and their analogues. Once such a locus is challenged the category of 'being' as an intelligible unity external to 'knowledge' is challenged (rationalist epistemologies are capable of coping with this: identifying real and rational or unifying existence and knowledge as spirit). Discourses then become interpretable and intelligible only in terms of their own or other discourses' constructions and the categories of adequacy which they apply to them. One has in the absence of a privileged level ('experience', or 'reason' which imposes form on discourse) to accept the *difference* of the referents of discourse, the potential infinity of referents.

Epistemological discourses attribute definite forms of unity to the objects known, and this unity mirrors the definite and general form of the knowledge process. Thus, for example, empiricism involves the reduction of all objects existent to knowledge to those appropriable in 'experience'. Thus the 'objects' to which botany and physics are supposed to correspond have common attributes, existence to experience. The empiricist is forced to argue in the case of subatomic physics that the instruments which both produce and register certain types of particles are extensions of experience, means of 'seeing' an independent reality. Outside of epistemology what it is discourses and practices construct and refer to has no necessary common attributes; equally these constructions and referents are unintelligible except in and as discourse. This does not mean we have abolished the 'non-discursive', merely that we deny general attributes attached to this category and that we deny any non-discursive level of 'experience' or 'consciousness'. Let us take as an example of those practices discourses where the category of 'experience' appears most appropriate: botany, anatomy, and so on. These involve definite practices of observation and visual representation of plants, bodily structures, etc. But these practices can in no sense be said to be exemplifications of knowledge through 'experience'. 'Experience' as an epistemological category reduces these practices to the unity of interiorisation of the sensible reality of the objects by a subject. It supposes moreover a subject appropriate to 'experience' whose sensory faculties are receptive to the intelligibility of the objects. Discourses must interdict and distort experience and access to this intelligibility. But processes of observation and visual representation are specific; they involve discourse, definite technique and training. It is well-established in the history of the sciences that the seventeenth and eighteenth centuries produced a revolution in the observation and depiction of plants and animal structures. This has often been interpreted as an awakening of 'experience', the product of a new openness of mind and a willingness to discard dogmas. Central in the revolution in botany is the production of new classificatory systems which organise the vegetable kingdom as a homogenous space of relations and differences between forms: observation is placed within a new type of order and a distinct, primarily classificatory, practice. Observation is transformed in its technologies; the systematisation of representational technique to rendering differences and relations between aspects of plants, and its stabilisation through plates of a new standard of accuracy. What separates Linnaeus from the 'herbals', the collections of lore and observations about plants so popular in the sixteenth century, is not attention to experience (the herbals reveal a wealth of attention to plants, their effects and uses) but a new machine of observation, a new gaze-in-discourse. Wat is observed is not merely sign, nor are observational practices reducible to the texts which organise them. Foucault brilliantly demonstrated in *The Birth of the Clinic* that the clinical gaze is a complex socio-discursive event, but that, within the institution of the hospital and upon the new discursively constituted space of the body: it is a *gaze* none the less. Its radical specificity and its difference as gaze from the desire-in-the-eye of the voyeur, or the languid contemplation of the window shopper are hidden from us by the category of 'experience'.

Rudolf Wittkower in a brilliant essay on the representation of 'monsters' demonstrated that the fantastic beings depicted in mediaeval and early modern texts represent no failure of 'observation' in the face of credulity and dogma. 'Monsters' are unintelligible except in terms of the status accorded to the texts of antiquity. Thus certain forms of visual 'representation' are hegemonised by verbal descriptions and are their semblance. They are the illustration of reports, and follow certain common discursive hemes established in antiquity. The changes in the zoological, anatomical and botanical practices of observation and depiction which abolished *these* monsters (it did not prevent the installation of *others*, as the history of depiction of human races stands witness) is a mutation in discourse and technique and not the installation of an originary 'experience'.

To those who reply that monsters did not 'really' exist I reply that 'monsters' never do, they are always the fallacies of ancestors and fears of children. The real question is the 'monsters' we cannot see because we believe in them. The potentiality of *difference* in the constructs of practices and the referents discourses speak of explodes the 'non-discursive' as a unitary category. What is constructed and referred to has no necessary unity and the attributes of constructs and referents differ with the type of operations involved. The obvious riposte to this is the change of 'relativism'. But relativism is only possible and pernicious *within epistemology*, as a general doctrine about the knowledge-being relation. The relativist argues that all statements and practices are equivalent relative to an (impossible or unattainable) concept of adequate knowledge, that is, correspondence to or appropriate of its objects. There are no general criteria of adequacy or truth. Hence the question – how do we know that statement is true? – and the paradox of relativism as epistemological doctrine. We would argue that discourses and practices *do* employ the criteria of appropriateness or adequacy (not of epistemological validity) but these are specific to the objectives of definite bodies of discourse and practice. None will pass muster as a general criterion of validity, but there is no knowledge process *in general* and, therefore, no necessity for such a criterion. Techniques of criticism of biblical texts are of no use in garage mechanics. Questions of priority and relation in the Gospels, of the state of wear of a gearbox elicit different types of tests and disputes about them. The referents and constructs, Gospels, motor cars, depend on conditions which differ, so do criteria and tests. Tests, etc., develop within the discourses and practices to which they relate and are subject to dispute. *As tests* they are radically different, they seek to establish or challenge different things according to the objectives and circumstances of the practice in question. The equivalence of relativism is not the problem. Adequacy or appropriateness is always a determinate question with determinate and variable means of its posing. It is a general question only for epistemology.

2 Problems and Advances in the Theory of Ideology

PREFATORY REMARKS

This chapter began as a talk given at the first Communist University of Cambridge (1976). It was transcribed and produced in pamphlet form by Cambridge University Communist Party. The reason for reprinting it here is that although it is almost exclusively expositional it does emphasise and clarify a number of points in Althusser's work which are frequently overlooked or which are found difficult to follow, especially the concept of the 'imaginary relation'. The pamphlet enjoyed considerable success as an introduction and several readers suggested to me that it should be more readily available.

It is printed here as transcribed; no attempt has been made to eliminate the forms associated with oral presentation. It has in consequence a casual rather than a rigorous mode of argument.

The title of my talk today is 'Problems in the Marxist theory of ideology'. I am going to talk specifically about one set of discussions of Marxist theory of ideology, which is found in certain of the works of Louis Althusser. Now this may seem to some somewhat partisan, since there is a great deal of writing on the Marxist theory of ideology apart from Althusser's contribution. However, I think Althusser has made a number of significant advances in trying to deal with the problem of what is called 'ideology', and a number of important criticisms of previous theoretical positions. My talk will be an expositional one; its object will be to deal with what I think Althusser's advances are, and in doing this I want to try and say where Althusser has advanced over previous Marxist discussions of the problems of ideology. Previous discussions will be considered in that context.

(I) IDEOLOGY AS DISTORTED REPRESENTATION

I want to deal with Althusser's theoretical advances in the form of a number of theses; for those who have read Althusser on the theory of ideology, these theses will be somewhat familiar. I would say that the general effect of Althusser's position is to attempt to combat the idea that ideology is falsity, and to challenge what I would call the sociological mode of interpretation of ideology, that is, to analyse ideology through the social positions of people who are conceived as embodying the 'outlook' of these positions. Let me start with the first Althusserian thesis: *Ideology is not a distorted representation of reality*. This I do not doubt will appear to some people to be scandalous. It will become clearer when we consider the concept of the imaginary relation. But for the moment let us see what criticisms Althusser makes of conceptions in which ideology is a distorted representation of the real world. These conceptions of ideology as a misrepresentation of reality involve certain important theoretical consequences, and I shall briefly dwell on these.

Firstly, this position involves a conception of knowledge as being formed through the consciousness or experience of human subjects; ideology is then a distorted perception of reality by these knowing subjects. But this is exactly the classical empiricist conception of knowledge, i.e. knowledge is derived from a subject's experience of an object which is exterior to it. So in order for the thesis that ideology is a distorted recognition of reality to be sustained, it must be argued that the process of knowledge described by empiricism is a real process, though it leads to 'false' results. This is the first basic theoretical consequence: Ideology is knowledge derived from experience. This is a position which many people, including 'structuralists' like Jacques-Alain Miller, in his paper 'The Function of Theoretical Training' and Jacques Rancière, in 'The Concept of "critique" and the "Critique of Political Economy"', have actually taken up.

The second theoretical consequence is that the experiences the subject has are mediated by the social position of the subject. In consequence society must be conceived as a system of places, points of perception, and these places have experience-effects: if one is a finance capitalist, one will see the world differently than if one is an artisan. To use a metaphor from astronomy we can regard this as being like the difference between one observer observing celestial phenomena given to experience while standing on the earth, and another observing from a position on the sun. Marx uses this metaphor once or twice in *Capital*. Ideology is therefore a function of the structure of reality itself; the places that are created by social relations generate the ideologies that follow from them, through the mechanism of experience. It follows that any system can only generate certain definite forms of ideology: any social formation like, for example, capitalism or feudalism can only create certain kinds of experience-effects because of the structure of 'places' in it, capitalist and worker, serf and lord, etc. These represent, as in the astronomical metaphor, different points of view of the totality.

From this position follows the reductionist or sociologistic mode of analysis of ideology. The key thing in this type of analysis of ideology is the determination of the position of the subject. This means that the practice of interpretation involves the analysis of looking at the subject's social position, because ideology is a form of misrepresentation of the real determined by the position of the subject in the real. Reality is the primary determinant of ideology, it is the origin of ideology because it creates the position from which the experience is generated, and because it determines it: it is the truth of ideology. It is the point of truth that contradicts the falsity that it itself creates. Ideology is an experience created by the real, so we must know how that experience is created by the real in order to understand it. The analysis of the origin, returning to the social position of the subject, is the primary form of analysis. And a return to the origin is a return to truth. Because we take the point of view of reality itself, we understand the limits in the forms of 'knowledge' generated by partial positions or standpoints subjects have inside reality. To use the astronomical metaphor again, we must as it were move from the point of view of the observer seeing apparent phenomena to the analysis of the structure of planetary spaces and their motions. You can see here that the reality or truth of ideology is outside it in the prior determination or the creation of a system of places. It follows that reductionism is a legitimate mode of analysis. The subject mediates the experience of the place – it is the structure of 'places' which generates experience-effects. To look for the social position of a subject is a legitimate means of analysis of the ideas subjects hold, whether those subjects be individual subjects or classes.

So, this reductionist mode of interpretation involves on the one hand sociologism; the subject is in effect reduced to its place. If one is a capitalist one is a personification of capital, an embodiment of a place. On the other hand it involves an essentialism, in that one crucial category *not* reducible to the system of places is that of experience. Experience is conceived as an essential attribute or faculty of the subject, who may be either an individual or a class. A system of places is presumed and then subjects are somehow parachuted into them; they just happen to land with all the faculties necessary for experience. In fact they land with their sociological recognition-apparatus all ready before they receive their social position. This recognition apparatus is the faculty of experience. So the notion that empiricism is a real process of knowledge and not merely a theory of knowledge is necessary to this position because you will note that, as in empiricism, you have to postulate the idea of a knowing subject with a capacity for experience and the faculty of experience.

I have presented this thesis at some length because I think it is central to reductionist theories of ideology. There are two basic variants of this thesis that ideology is a distorted representation of reality. One is what Althusser calls historicism. In considering historicism, we shall take the example of Lukács, for reasons of familiarity. In Lukács' *History and Class Consciousness* the key modulation of the argument is that the subjects of experience are class subjects and that there is no 'disembodied' or 'objective' knowledge of reality independent of class standpoints. The subject who knows reality is actually the class subject which is dominant in the process of constructing history. This subject knows reality because it makes it, and it only knows it fully if it makes it in a non-alienated mode. So that the first subject really to know social relations will be the proletariat. This is because the proletariat, in the process of constructing socialism will be the first class to make history without alienation. This subject will recognise the truth of social relations in so far as they can be comprehended at all. Here we have the position that there is a true consciousness, a subject whose knowledge is adequate to the social totality because this class subject is in the process of constructing and reconstructing the totality. It is the subject of history. This subject transcends alienation in a revolutionary praxis and therefore transcends the limitations of points of view, so that knowledge through the experience of this class subject is adequate to the totality it experiences.

The second variant of this position is what is often called 'structuralism'.

Two classic examples of the conception of ideology, assumed in the astronomical metaphor, are found in the works by Rancière and Miller mentioned before. As we have seen, this conception entails that there is a structure of places which have experience-effects, and that empiricism describes a real process of knowledge. But there is a key difference between the historicist position and the 'structuralist' position. The latter does not conceive of a 'true subject' of history; since it denies that there can be true knowledge through the experience of a subject. All knowledge by a subject is empiricist and therefore inadequate, ideological. All subjects whose knowledge of the social world is derived from experience are condemned to ideology (because experience is necessarily empiricist). To my mind, Rancière presents convincing arguments that this is the position adopted by Marx in sections of *Capital*.

One has to take Rancière's arguments about the theory of fetishism in *Capital* seriously, because if he is right, then Marx is also a 'structuralist', i.e. at least in those sections of *Capital* which Rancière deals with (the very parts of the work generally considered to be the most Hegelian), Marx had a structuralist theory of ideology.

What I have done here is to present the main criticism of the position that ideology is a distorted representation of reality, the criticism being that it presupposes that knowledge really is derived from the experience of a subject. In his philosophical work, Althusser argues that empiricism is an impossible epistemology, an inadequate conception of knowledge. For him, it cannot therefore designate a real process of knowledge.

(II)   THE MATERIALITY OF IDEOLOGY

The second thesis runs as follows: *Ideology is not ideal or spiritual.* There are no really good English substitutes for the words 'ideal' or 'spiritual' available for use in theoretical contexts. What Althusser is trying to do with this thesis is to displace the opposition or couple, ideas: matter. A great deal of the orthodox Marxist theory of ideology is the theoretical residue of a fight between idealist and materialist philosophies of history. It was a fight which Marx and Engels, in their break from Left Hegelianism and Feuerbachism were forced to engage in. A classic example is *The German Ideology*. Recognising this, Marx said that *The German Ideology* was a labour he and Engels had to undertake, which they had gone beyond. No doubt it was necessary to fight the idealist-materialist battle in the philosophy of history; however, Marx later rejected the vulgar materialism of his initial positions in this struggle.

Althusser insists that ideology does not consist of 'ideas' as opposed to matter. For these categories return us to the classic dualist conception of the human subject as a combination of matter (body) and ideas (mind or consciousness). Materialism in these terms is simply the mirror image of idealism. Ideas are not to be counterposed to matter or reality. For Althusser, ideas are real and not 'ideal' because they are always inscribed in social practices and are expressed in objective social forms (languages, rituals, etc.). As such they have definite effects. Althusser asserts the materiality of ideology; in other words, he uses the thesis of materialism to upturn the matter: ideas opposition. Ideologies are not simply reflections in some realm of 'ideas' of social relations; they are part of social relations.

Ideology is what Althusser calls an instance of the social totality. What Althusser means by an 'instance' is that there is a specific practice involved in the instance and that the instance is the way in which this practice is articulated into the social totality. There are three main practices conceived in Althusser's work: economic practice (transformation of nature within social relations); political practice (the struggle to transform social relations themselves); and ideological practice (I shall explain what this is in a moment). Nevertheless ideology is a practice which is articulated in social formations in relation to the other practices, in a hierarchy of determinations. Ideology is a set of social practices and social representations and rituals. It is a structure of social relationships which is both determined by other social relations and which has a determining effect on them. So the analysis of ideology is the analysis of social relations, not of a reflection of social relations in some world of ideas. What Althusser tries to do here is to get away from the position that somehow reality is in your stomach or somewhere beyond the cosmos. 'Ideas' do not exist as spiritual entities. Ideologies are social relations, they are as real as the economy. The notion that somehow the economy is primary in the sense that it alone is the real foundation of everything else – (it is 'matter') – entails a retreat into philosophical materialism. Althusser argues that historical materialism conceives of the social totality as a hierarchy of instances and these are as real as one another; they merely have different relative weights in determining the whole. This thesis of being determined and determining is what Althusser means by the concept of over determination.

In essence Althusser's thesis that ideology is not spiritual is an attack on the kind of materialistic interpretation of history in which ideas are epiphenomenal. We should recall that it was this kind of vulgar materialism that led Marx to leave the 'Marxist' camp, in words at least. This Marxist camp wasn't Marx's camp. It was the camp of materialistic interpreters of history, who took 'matter' (a technicist conception of the economy) as a primary fact. When Marx said he was not a Marxist he was defending historical materialism against vulgar materialism.

(III) IDEOLOGY, HISTORY AND THE IMAGINARY

The third thesis is a famous one and is probably the most misinterpreted of all Althusser's theses. The third thesis that Althusser puts forward is: *ideology has no history*. Surely this is a scandal; how can ideology have no history? Well, as with many scandals, scandalous words are being used to explain reasonable things. This thesis amounts to nothing more than a thesis of the universality of the ideological instance in the social totality. The theory of the social totality deals with three instances – economic, political, ideological – two of which are universal: economy and ideology. Politics is not universal because Althusser, being a Communist, believes in a communist society in which the domination of man by man gives way to the administration of things. So there is no mystery as to why the political disappears. Obviously, why ideology continues requires some argument. The reason why he argues this is so is because of the structure of all social totalities. There will never be a totality in which the human subjects who live in social relations can comprehend them through experience because social totalities do not exist in a form which is accessible to experience.

The subject is related to the totality through an 'imaginary' relation. This 'imaginary' relation of subjects to their conditions of existence is the foundation of ideology. We shall consider in a

moment the concept of the imaginary. Before proceeding to this
we shall make some remarks as to its status. It is the central
concept in the Althusserian theory of ideology, and if one does
not deal in detail with this concept one cannot comprehend the
theory. Most of the critiques of Althusser's theory of ideology are
based on the idea that it is a positivist theory of ideology in which
ideology misrepresents the real. Hence it appears scandalous that
Althusser asserts the universality of ideology. Critics of Althusser
like Geras and Kolakowski, who make much of his theory of
ideology and of the autonomy of science from the social
formation, simply do not deal with the concept of the imaginary
relation. Yet this is the central concept in Althusser's theory of
ideology.

Althusser argues that there is no end to the imaginary relation
by which men live their relations to their conditions of existence.
The notion of the end of ideology involves the idea that it is
possible for there to be a true consciousness of social relations, and
in turn this involves the idea that social relations can exist in a
form in which they can be known in experience. So that
experience here corresponds to truth – it is the basis of an
adequate knowledge of social relations. The classic argument for
the notion of true consciousness, that is, that experience is
adequate to its object (that object being manifest truth), is the
1844 Manuscripts. In this text, Marx conceives the social relations
of communism purely in terms of spontaneous human intersubjectivity. Marx calls communist society 'concrete sensuous
human self-creation' and says that it is the solution to the 'riddle'
of history. History ceases to be a riddle because it no longer exists.
There is no history in communist society because there is concrete
sensuous human activity which is 'immediate' to itself, i.e. not
'mediated' by alienated social relations. History is the process of
man's realisation of his essence, and it proceeds through
alienation. Experience is adequate to the social relations of
communism because there is no longer alienation, and therefore
there is no 'riddle'. The concept of immediacy is necessary in this
case. Immediate social relations are ones which are spontaneous
between human subjects. Under communism, social relations are

dissolved into purely spontaneous intersubjective relations, spontaneous because not mediated by social forms which dominate human subjects and are outside their direct control. Only these immediate relations can be truly known through experience.

This thesis Althusser challenges as an historicist one. He argues that in historicist theories there is a correspondence between the knowledge of the subject and the object, through the mechanism of experience, because the subject is what he calls a constitutive subject. The subject constitutes what it knows, it is the origin of what it knows, and therefore experience is the return of the origin to itself. We must insist therefore that the subject is truly the origin of its social relations. Take the formula 'men make history'. If men 'make' history why does the 'falsity' of ideology distort their perceptions? Ideology represents the making of history in an alienated mode. Alienation is the displacement of immediacy, the creation of social relations which involve the mediation of the subject's product (history) to it in forms it does not recognise. Constitutivity is displaced, the subject is no longer constitutive of or to itself. Men are the authors of their social relations but the conditions under which they make them means that their product escapes them. Alienation is a necessary part of history. The end of alienation is the recognition by man of himself as origin of his social relations and true experience is the return of the origin to itself. Subject and object are one, and therefore there is a correspondence of knowledge with its object.

The thesis that one can dispense with ideology involves (if it is developed rigorously), the idea that social relations originate in the actions of human subjects who self-consciously know those actions and their consequences to be their own. The concept of a constitutive subject entails that the subject be an essence, a pure origin. The subject is origin – it can have no conditions of existence without ceasing to be constitutive. Constitutivity must further rely on the subject's experience as an adequate account of its nature (a super-subjective knowledge negates constitutivity). Because the subject is necessarily known through itself as knowing subject, historicism is committed either to an extreme idealism, or to the limits of knowledge entailed in empiricism. If the subject knows its essence through self-consciousness then this consciousness is the presence-to-itself of truth (this position is only credible with reference to God's knowledge; God is pure origin and questions as to the conditions of His existence are impertinent). If the subject simply experiences itself as object, it is caught in the classic empiricist 'problem of knowledge' (which Althusser considers to be a pseudo-problem). Self-consciousness is the subject's experience of itself as an object to itself. Even if it experiences itself as constitutive it has no knowledge of itself (of its nature and existence) other than this experience. The subject must either trust experience (Cartesian double-think) or collapse into scepticism. The subject ever-always exists as a given to itself and to knowledge. Historicism is forced to make the nature of its most important category (subject) a mystery, a given beyond knowledge.

(IV) THE CONCEPT OF THE IMAGINARY RELATION

The fourth thesis is the most important one: *ideology is not false consciousness*. Althusser insists, and this takes us back to the first point, that ideology is not a distorted representation of reality. Althusser further insists that ideology is not a representation of reality at all. What ideology represents is men's lived relation to their conditions of existence. This lived relation is Althusser insists, an 'imaginary' relation. Now what does it mean to say that the subject lives his relation to his conditions of existence in an 'imaginary' mode? This word 'imaginary' is a metaphor borrowed from psycho-analysis (from Jacques Lacan). I am not going to go into the source of the borrowing but rather into what Althusser makes of it.

The imaginary modality of living is necessary because men's conditions of existence can never be given to them in experience. Hence the importance of the attack on the theory of ideology as experience. There cannot be any true or false *consciousness* because there is no basis for a correspondence between the experience of the subject and his social relations. This requires us to introduce the Althusserian concept of the social totality somewhat more rigorously than we have done heretofore. The social totality is conceived as a 'process without a subject'. What does this mean? It means essentially that the social totality is not a process constituted by a subject, and that subjects occupy a place in it other than origin or author.

This fourth thesis involves the point that was made in relation to the intersubjective theories, i.e. social relations are not reducible to intersubjective relations. This means that the subject lives in relation to the totality of its social conditions of existence in such a way that the subject can never simply recognise these conditions. This is because there are no essential subjects involved. The forms of subjectivity are conceived as both effects of and supports of the process. The relation of subject to the process (what the subject is) is determined by the process and the subject as a support of this process becomes a part of the totality. The totality forms subjects (because it provides their conditions of existence) in such a way that they can never 'recognise' it. The imaginary is the form in which the subject 'lives' its relation both to the (absent) totality (its conditions of existence) and to its existence as a subject. The conditions of existence of the subject are both present and absent to it. They are present, in the sense that the structure of the totality determines the 'place' of the subject in it, and therefore the conditions the imaginary must articulate. They are absent, in that the totality is not an essential totality, united by some inner essence, its elements linked to one another in principle, but on the contrary, the totality is present in and as its effects. The 'imaginary' relation is a (relatively autonomous) element of the totality – determined and determining. The totality (the 'matrix' of the instances) determines the 'space' of the imaginary as one of its instances. The imaginary is a specific articulation of that space (it relates the supports to the process). Because there is no essential whole given in advance to the 'imaginary' and 'pictured' in it, the imaginary is what it is (it is a specific effectivity). The relation of the subjects to the process established in the imaginary is not given elsewhere: it is not a *pars totalis*, it does not reflect the relations it articulates. The whole is not present – i.e. manifest – in the imaginary; all that is present in the imaginary is the relation which the imaginary is and determines. As a consequence, the subject has a relation to the process which, although determined by the process, does not represent in an expressive form the totality of its determinations.

It is important to introduce the notion of 'as if' here. The imaginary essentially consists in the idea that the subject lives its relation to its conditions of existence *as if* it were a subject. It is a subject because it exists in the realm of the 'as if', but it lives these relations *as if* they were true. It would be too simple to say that subjects live in the supposition that they are constitutive. The 'as if' involves the position that subjectivity is both constitutive and non-constitutive. Subjects do not constitute their social relations, they are not the origin of their social relations. But they live them in a different mode to that, and they live them 'as if' they did do more than that. This means that they are subjects because they are constituted 'as if' they constituted themselves.

Let us say in relation to this concept of 'as if' that what the subject does in living things 'as if', really does have effects. So that if you will permit me a bit of dialectics . . . the subject lives 'as if' it were a subject, and through the 'as if' it really does have a determinate effect. So that although the subject is not a constitutive subject, and the imaginary is overdetermined by the totality of conditions of existence, the imaginary in turn overde-termines that totality and becomes part of it. So that we do not have a truth/falsity, illusion/reality opposition here. The imag-inary relation is a relation of the totality (it is part of the totality) and has a determining effect in it. It is not determinant in the last instance but is effective as an instance. So the imaginary is not a reflection, it doesn't *reflect* the conditions of existence of men but *is* their relation to them. And it is not false, it is absolutely not falsity. The imaginary does not represent anything other than what it is, and it cannot be false since it is not an idea or conception of things, but it is a part of social relations which has a definite effect. In living 'as if', subjects do not live in illusion, this 'as if' is the *reality* of their existence as subjects.

With his concepts of the 'ideological instance' and the 'imaginary relation', Althusser opens up the possibility of a whole region of social relations relatively autonomous from the economy, and with a (potential) effect on the totality. Ideology in this conception has serious political implications since it raises the prospect of 'ideological struggle' as a distinct arena of political struggle. It raises the prospect of changes in the forms of the 'imaginary' producing changes in the relations of subjects to the totality. (It might be said that he also closes it again since the 'imaginary' is an effect of the totality, a product of the action of its structure: how is it to be changed since subjects are effects of the process?). The question whether ideological struggle is possible and does have an effect is a politically important one. If ideological struggle does have an effect on social relations we shall begin to think about what ideological practices there are, how they can be transformed, and what the conditions of doing so are. If ideology is a reflection of social position and falsity, or illusion, for all but the proletariat, then ideological struggle is limited, to proclaiming a new world view, whose victory is pre-given. We should, therefore, return to Christopher Caudwell and take it from there, recognising along the way that Freud, Einstein and Joyce are bourgeois junk. These seem to be the choices; there is not a midway position. Those are the alternatives: either taking ideological struggle seriously, because 'ideology' is a relatively autonomous arena of social reations; or taking up a position that ideology is a reflection of social relations and, in its bourgeois forms, illusion. Reductionist analyses lead to a class essentialist and economistic practice in relation to ideology, a practice which is sectarian and self-defeating (ideological effects are given in class experience).

To many orthodox Marxists, it may well be the case, for example, that a great many of the things the Women's Movement do appear to be absurd. The practices in question have the ideological recognition effect of absurdity: 'Why do they do silly things like that? That won't solve "the real", economic and political, problems.' But though a great many campaigns in which the Women's Movement engages may not be terribly effective in promoting socialist politics directly, they may be important in creating the basis on which an important section of the population is prepared to take socialist agitation seriously. The struggles involved are for the removal of real 'ideological' obstacles, social practices not 'illusions'. Willingness to recognise that ideology is not a matter of 'consciousness' (false or otherwise) might change many Marxists' attitudes to struggles of this type. It might make it possible for the Left to offer such movements (badly needed) political leadership, rather than opportunist tolerance and sloganising. I think we must take seriously Althusser's case that forms of 'ideological struggle' may have positive political effects, and that there is an area of 'ideological social relations' which is relatively autonomous from the economic and political which is an area of specific political practices.

(V) THE CONCEPT OF THE IMAGINARY AND THE SCIENCE-IDEOLOGY DISTINCTION

The concept of the imaginary is an extremely problematic concept. I am not going to hide the fact that I think it is a metaphor and that a good deal of its substance evaporates when you look closely at it. I have examined the Althusserian theory of ideology as social relations and I have not dealt with Althusser's theory of ideology in relation to his theory of knowledge. Now I have done this quite deliberately because I think that what Althusser has to say about 'ideological social relations' is revolutionary in its implications, turning Marxism away from reductionist and sociologistic modes of handling ideology, whereas Althusser's theory of knowledge seems to me to be much more problematic. Although the two are connected I think that what Althusser has done in the theory of ideology can be considered relatively independently of his theory of knowledge. But as it were to subvert that, I will say that there is a very definite connection between the two, and that is in relation to the concept of the imaginary. The imaginary is vital for Althusser's conception of ideological and scientific knowledge. This is because ideology is always a form of the creation of recognition, i.e. the imaginary always creates forms of recognition, which are the basis of the lived relationship. The imaginary is a part of the totality. All recognition is necessarily coupled with misrecognition. Recognition is always a form of the imaginary relation, so that the analysis of ideology as a social relation provides a connection with the epistemological distinction between ideological and scientific knowledges. Ideological knowledges and theoretical ideologies are elaborations of what Althusser calls practical social ideologies (what we have been talking about so far). These ideological knowledges represent the elaboration or reflection of the forms of recognition that the subject has in the imaginary relation, so they elaborate the forms of recognition which form the imaginary relation in which the subject lives. Recognition entails misrecognition, it is a definite mode of the imaginary which does not reflect the totality to men. Ideological knowledges, as a consequence of this point of departure, are necessarily closed, and are condemned to repeat the closure which constitutes the recognition structure. They are condemned to repeat the forms of the imaginary in which the subject exists and lives as a subject. Sciences and ideologies are distinguished by the openness and closure of their discursive structures. That is, they are distinguished by the modes in which they develop and pose problems. The imaginary effects closure. Science, which comes into existence through the epistemological break, breaks the space of recognition. The epistemological break is a shattering of closure and hence creates the possibility of openness, because it breaks the forms of recognition. This entails the notion that science (and this is why Althusser insists on the autonomy of science in the social formation) is a process without a subject. This process begins with a critique of the forms of recognition, and goes beyond subjectivity and the imaginary, so that because it is a process without a subject it transcends the imaginary relation and therefore transcends closure. The autonomy of scientific knowledge from the social formation is argued in terms of the autonomy of scientific knowledge from the imaginary relation. This is the crucial point; Althusser does not believe that scientists sit on clouds. The autonomy involved is the autonomy from the imaginary, the critique breaking the imaginary space.

Science knows ideology to be ideological; it does not know it to be illusory or false. Science as Althusser tries to develop it is not an illusion/reality distinction. There are a lot of problems with that, and I do not subscribe to Althusserian epistemology. But I am prepared to put up the best possible case for Althusser. This is because his position is far more sophisticated than any of the critiques that have been produced of it. Ideology is not illusory for the reason we have given before; it is not illusion, it is not falsity, because how can something which has effects be false? It may derive from forms of the imaginary but it is not false. It would be like saying a black pudding is false, or a steamroller is false. Althusser argues that it is only because science transcends the imaginary relation that it can know what ideology is. How is it possible to defend this position? The answer is that it is not the theory of science which has discovered the imaginary, that somehow the epistemological searchlight has been switched on and we find ourselves living in a world of sophistry and illusion which we are about to commit to the flames. Althusser's position on his own epistemology is that it is possible only within Marxist philosophy. What it is that enables epistemology to deal with the theory of ideology is precisely a particular science, Marxism, and not simply any epistemological theory. This epistemological theory that Althusser advances has the concept of ideology it does, precisely because this epistemology is derived from Marxism.

Althusser would argue that the science/ideology distinction is a strong one, precisely because it rests on a particular science, Marxism, and particularly upon the Marxist theory of ideology. The distinction between science and ideology depends not simply on the concepts of Marxist philosophy, but upon those of historical materialism. A lot of the criticisms of Althusser's epistemology fail to recognise this. For example, how is it possible to reconcile the specificity of forms of proof employed in particular sciences with the claims of a general theory concerning the difference between scientific and ideological discourse? The answer is a relatively simple one – precisely because the general theory is derived from a particular science, namely historical materialism. The concept of ideology involved is a scientific, not a philosophical one. A major difficulty with a lot of this, is that the way Althusser develops his argument involves a conjuring trick. He gives us to believe that the theory of ideology has always been there, i.e. that historical materialism contains an already elaborated theory of ideology. Whereas the theory of ideology he in fact depends on is his own.

(VI) CONCLUSION

If one takes Althusser's epistemology and the defences that can be made of it seriously, one must take his theory of ideology seriously. It seems to me that this theory merits thorough analysis. It is, I would argue, the first significant advance in this area of Marxism since the early twentieth century; all the other basic positions have certainly been around since Lukács wrote *History and Class Consciousness*. What Althusser has done in criticising the earlier positions is absolutely central. He has challenged the reductionist and sociologistic mode of analysis of ideologies; challenged the notion of an 'end' to ideology in true consciousness: challenged the notion of ideology as false consciousness; and challenged the idea that ideology is an unreal or illusory reflection. He has generated the problem of the investigation of a definite area of social relations which is relatively independent of the economy and of politics and which has significant political consequences.

3 Althusser and the Theory of Ideology

Althusser's writings on ideolgy[1] have transformed a virtually moribund region of Marxist theory. Althusser has challenged certain central aspects of the classic Marxist theories of ideology and he has attempted to introduce a new set of problems. Althusser's challenge consists in essence in rejecting the sociologistic and reductionist methods of analysis of ideology dominant in Marxism. His attempt to change the terms of the problem of 'ideology' consists in the rejection of the conception of ideologies as reflections of social reality in consciousness and the substitution of a conception of ideology as a structure of social relations no less 'real' than the economic and the political and articulated with them.

I have considered Althusser's criticism of other theories of ideology in greater detail elsewhere.[2] Here I shall merely make some limited points to situate the discussion of his paper, 'Ideology and Ideological State Apparatuses', which forms the bulk of this chapter. Althusser's challenge to the classic theories of ideology is part of a broader rejection of humanism and historicism. Althusser rejects two positions hitherto central in Marxist theories (they are positions taken by Marx in *The German Ideology*): (i) that ideology is a false representation of the *real*: (ii) that ideology is a distorted *reflection in consciousness* of real social relations. Althusser challenges the notion that ideology is a 'false consciousness' of reality because it entails the conception of knowledge as the experience of a subject: false consciousness is true consciousness in blinkers. In empiricism objects are knowable through recognition; in the subject/object structure experience either corresponds to the nature of the object or misrecognises it. The object is in principle knowable, the non-correspondence of experience with its object can be explained by a defect in the subject (insanity, hallucination), or by the special circumstances in which the object presents itself (it generates an 'appearance'). False consciousness is explained in Marxism by the *relation* of the subject to the object. Reality (the object) determines the place of the subject within it and, therefore, the conditions of its experience of it. Reality determines the *content* of ideology; it generates false recognitions of itself by subjecting subjects to circumstances in which their experience is distorted. Reality is the *origin* of ideology because it creates the different 'places', class positions, from which subjects view it. To know ideology is ideological is to perceive reality itself. To determine the position of the subject in the real is, therefore, to recognise both the content of ideology and its source. Once the social position of the subject is known, the nature of its consciousness and its source can be determined. Sociologism (reducing ideology to an effect of the social position of the subject who expounds it) is a legitimate procedure if knowledge is conceived as experience and if society is considered as a system of places conditioning that experience into 'class outlooks'. Althusser denies that knowledge through experience is possible and, therefore, that class positions automatically generate experience-effects, 'class outlooks'. The social position of the subject is not the *origin* of its ideological position; ideology has conditions of existence which cannot be 'read off' from the place of the subject in the relations of production.

Althusser's paper 'Ideology and Ideological State Apparatuses' (ISAs) is his attempt to state what these conditions of existence are. Althusser argues contrary to the empiricist conception that there are not given subjects with an experience of the real. Subjects are not essential but are constituted. There is no 'social reality' which can be *present* to experience. Men's conditions of existence cannot be manifest to them and in consequence they live their relation to these (absent) conditions in an imaginary mode. They live them in an imaginary presence, 'as if' they were given. Ideology is a representation of this 'imaginary' modality by which men live their relation to the (absent) totality of their conditions of existence. Ideology is not 'consciousness', it is a representation of the 'imaginary'. This 'imaginary' relation is not the experience or consciousness of an already constituted subject, it is in the imaginary that the subject is formed as a subject. The subject becomes what it is through the imaginary relation, it cannot be the pure subject of the empiricist notion of experience because it is *formed* through a definite structure of recognition.

Althusser's rejection of the reductionist mode of interpretation of ideology leads to its replacement by another conception of the relation of the ideological to the social totality. Ideological social relations are articulated within a system of ISAs and these apparatuses serve to reproduce the relations of production. They are organs of the state but are not necessarily included within the constitutional form of the state. They are unified by a common function, the reproduction of the dominant relations of production.

Althusser's theory, as presented in the ISAs paper, falls into two related components:

(i) the theory of the ISAs, ideology is articulated as a system of institutions unified by the ideology of the dominant class, these institutions form and condition subjects to accept the dominant relations of production;
(ii) the theory of the formation of subjects through the mechanism of 'interpellation', the constitution of the subject in the recognition structure of the 'imaginary'.

In this chapter, Althusser's theory will be subjected to criticism. Criticism not in the service of the classical problematics but in order to extend Althusser's challenge to these reductionist conceptions of ideology. This criticism is necessary because Althusser's position in the ISAs represents a failure to break with economism and class essentialism.

In the first section (A) the pertinence of the 'problem' to which the ISAs represent an answer will be considered. In the second section (B) the concept of ISA itself will be examined. The next two sections (C and D) will consider the notion of the imaginary relation of the subject to its conditions of existence and Althusser's explanation of the constitution of the subject through the recognition structure of the imaginary. In the final section (E) the implications of the concept of 'representation' and its use by Althusser will be considered.

A THE PROBLEM OF THE REPRODUCTION OF THE RELATIONS OF PRODUCTION

Althusser's paper 'Ideology and Ideological State Apparatuses' represents his attempt to develop a theory of ideological social relations.

1 *The level of analysis*

Althusser makes much of what he calls 'the point of view of reproduction', a position he claims to derive from Marx's *Capital*. Althusser uses this 'point of view' to pose the problem of the 'reproduction of the relations of production'. The problem is that, given the level of generality of the analysis, this reproduction can only be converted into a functional imperative and apparatuses assigned to perform this function. The question of reproduction posed by Althusser is equivalent to the question 'how is it possible for capitalist social relations to exist?' No general answer can be given to this question which is *not* functionalist.

An index of the functional nature of Althusser's problem is the relation between the reproduction function and the agency which performs it. The agency can be conceived as a means to the fulfilment of a functional end. This means has no determinant effect on the form for which it is functional. It merely performs the function of maintenance or reproduction. It can be conceived therefore strictly as a support of the function. The function or functional end is universal; the agencies arise in particular social forms as conditional means of its performance. This can be seen in Althusser's treatment of the switch from the church/family couple, functional for reproduction of the relations of production in feudalism, to the school/family couple, functional for the reproduction of the relations of production in capitalism.

Althusser recognises what he calls the 'abstraction' of this analysis in the postscript. He argues that the mechanisms advanced by him to perform this function of reproduction depend for their realisation on concrete conditions, not given in discourse, which involve the class struggle and which will be determined in their effects by this struggle. In other words Althusser makes use of the abstract/concrete distinction to attempt to rectify the problems of generality of his analysis. A general functional mechanism is modified in its effects by the 'the concrete'. This abstract/concrete distinction is an impossible one. The functional mechanism which Althusser advances depends upon a certain discursive question, 'the reproduction of the relations of production'. It exists as such only as a result of the functionalist mode of posing the question. Althusser seeks to counteract the theoretical effects of this mechanism (functionalism) by reference to its inhibition by 'concrete' conditions. In effect, to rectify a problem in discourse by reference to the non-discursive. However, these 'concrete' conditions and the general mechanism are merely *brought together* in the pages of Althusser's discourse, there is no attempt to relate them theoretically. Indeed, they could not be – if Althusser's mechanism is 'abstract' then it can have no effects which can be counteracted, if it is not 'abstract' then it must be analysed in the same way as the class struggle. Althusser's problems stem from the recognition that the theory cannot specify that the agency it assigns to function *does* actually perform this function (the ultra-functionalist or structuralist has no need of the contradictory notion of the 'concrete'); this would be to give the structure necessarily for all time its own conditions of existence. This would be to retreat to the worst excesses of *Reading Capital*. However, the functionalist problem that Althusser has created requires such universal or general answers.

Althusser can only overcome the problem by a retreat into the, incoherent, supposition of 'concrete' conditions.

2 The pertinence of the 'problem'

Althusser's problem 'how is the reproduction of the relations of production secured?' (ISAs, p. 141) is a curious one. It represents a misreading of *Capital*. Althusser argues that in *Capital* vol. II, Marx analyses the reproduction of the *means* of production. Marx is concerned to do both more than this and less than this. In vol. II Marx is concerned to show how the relations of commodity production *can* resolve themselves into the distribution of the conditions of production; how the product is circulated between the classes, the branches and the departments involved in production in such a way that production can be renewed. This mechanism takes place by means of these relations of production (wage labour, profit, commodity circulation). These relations are, to use a phrase of Althusser's, although not in its structuralist sense, 'present in their effects'. In order that labour power be reproduced, that means of production are obtained, creditors are paid, etc., relations of wage labour, commodity purchase and sale, payment of interest, etc. must take place. If the conditions of production are distributed in capitalist forms, by means of the generalised circulation of commodities (including wage labour) then the relations of production are reproduced. The relations of production reproduce themselves in distributing the conditions of production to enterprises. Wage labourers purchase their means of subsistence, capitalists of department II purchase their means of production from capitalists of department I. Wage labour, capital, credit-interest and rent reproduce themselves as relations of production by being the forms in which the economy is reproduced.

The non-reproduction of the relations of production involves definite political and economic practices which *construct* other relations. This involves different questions from the one Althusser poses. These questions concern the conditions of existence of these practices of destruction and construction. No general answer, derivable from the general form of the relations of production, can be given to these questions – such an answer would be a general theory of transition.[3] Equally, there can be no general theory of the maintenance of capitalism. The relations of production are not *reproduced* except by existing – through their role in economic reproduction – there is no special agency which secures their existence as such. To 'reproduce' the relations is to reproduce capitalism. But we have argued that no general answer can be given to the question 'how is it possible that capitalist relations of production can continue to exist?' To analyse the forms of existence or supersession of capitalist social relations is to theorise definite capitalist social formations and the determinants of the conjunctures which are the forms of their existence or transformation.

Althusser poses the question of the general mechanism ('ideology') by which the 'reproduction of the relations of production' can be secured, the answer he gives to this question is an apparatus the effect of which, if it does function, is equivalent to the securing of the conditions of existence of capitalist production. He attempts to counteract this functionalism by adding to this 'abstract' scheme the 'class struggle' as its concrete conditions of realisation.

3 *Althusser's answer*

Althusser's answer to the question of the reproduction of the relations of production reveals the functionalist manner in which it was posed. He resolves the problem of 'the reproduction of the relations of production' into the distribution of agents suitably equipped as 'supports' for the 'places' of the social division of labour, the 'places' are thus provided with subjectivities adequate and appropriate to them. (In *Capital* this relation of the subject to the process is accomplished by automatic mechanisms at the level of the economy; by the supposition of subjects with the faculty of experience who derive their capacities for action through recognising the phenomenal forms that the economy generates.) Althusser has equated the *relations of production* with the distribution of agents to 'places' in the social division of labour. The relations of production are conceived as *relations between agents*, 'personifications', to use Marx's phrase, of the social positions they occupy.

Althusser makes three related errors: (i) the equation of the relations of production with the functions assigned to economic agents in the social division of labour (capitalist, wage labourer); (ii) the confusion of places in the social division of labour with the divisions of the occupational structure; (iii) the equation of economic agents with human subjects.

First, the relations of production include not only agents but *forms of relation between agents*. Forms of circulation and exchange, for example. These forms have an objective existence and are not reproduced spontaneously by behaviours of the agents, Marx does not conceive the forms of circulation process in capitalism merely as a series of interrelations between subjects as exchanges generated through the correspondence of motivations of subjects. Marx, unlike his contemporary Menger and near-contemporary Böhm-Bawerk, did not conceive exchange as intersubjectivity. Thus to reproduce the agents is not to reproduce the forms of relations between them.

Moreover, *not all economic agents are human subjects*. Capital, for example, does not necessarily involve *capitalists*, persons who own the means of production as private property. 'Anonymous' unities of possession may represent capital on the prevailing social scale. The money funds involved in these capitals do not represent capital, that is the means of production, to those with a claim upon them (bank depositors, stockholders, policy holders, etc.). Hence corporate entities may be the social forms of effective possession of capital in the dominant branches of production and it is these forms which then represent the economic agent *capital*. These 'anonymous' enterprises are managed. That is, functionaries perform the function of direction of the means of production. Now it may be said that managers 'take the place of the capitalist'. However, it is the *enterprise* which is the economic subject: the level of possession and the form of economic operation. Managers are the supports of this economic subject. It is not merely a question of 'taking the place of . . .' – the existence of a supply of trained managers is not a sufficient condition for the reproduction of the enterprise. Enterprises are not reproduced by educating human subjects.

Further, the division of the labour force into categories and the relations of production do not correspond in capitalism. Classes and divisions of the labour force into functional groups are not the same thing. Capitalist production creates the conditions of existence of the following economic classes: wage labourers, capitals (industrial, commercial, interest-bearing and landed), petit bourgeois (independent producers, small capitals, etc.). These classes do not correspond to the divisions of the labour force: managerial/non-managerial, manual/non-manual, skilled/unskilled, etc. These latter may all be formerly wage labourers who do not own the means of production. The class of wage labourers formed by capitalist production includes all these divisions of the labour force. These divisions cannot be recuperated to the relations of production by the use of categories like productive and unproductive labour, or by assigning occupations the status of 'representatives' of capital or the collective labourer, etc. Ingenious as such attempts may be, they cannot consistently necessitate the diversity of forms of division of the labour force and reduce it to the simple dichotomy of the relations of production involved in wage labour. These practices 'distribute' the categories of the occupational structure to the places in the relations of production. Thus one occupation is considered to perform the 'function' of capital whilst another occupation is part of the collective labourer. Even if one accepts these practices of assignation and distribution, the problem remains that the divisions of the labour force other than those functionaries who direct the means of production in the service of capital are unexplained — the divisions of the labour force remain. These divisions of the labour force depend upon economic and other (which Althusser would call 'ideological') determinants that are not reducible to the relations of production *per se*. It is with these divisions of the labour force and their reproduction that Althusser is concerned in the ISAs paper and not with the relations of production. It is certainly the case that many of these divisions of the labour force are reproduced in part through the educational system, training being one of their determinants, but this is a different question from the one Althusser poses.

The social division of labour and the structure of the labour force are not the same thing. The sources of divisions of the labour force – the determinants of specialisation, forms of training, types of administration, 'management', etc. – are important questions which need to be investigated by Marxists. We are not suggesting that they are unproblematic. Althusser, however, does not pose or answer these questions. It should be noted that the divisions of the labour force which are influenced by the educational system (manual/non-manual, skilled/unskilled, managerial/non-managerial) exist in socialist countries also, for example the U.S.S.R. Whilst these divisions are not equivalent to the relations of production, it should not be thought that they are inconsequential for the development of the relations of production. The conditions of the displacement of these divisions should be investigated. It can be argued that these divisions rest not upon specific relations of production but upon what Marx calls the division of mental and manual labour and what he calls the division between town and country. These divisions cannot be conceived as solely the effects of the capitalist mode of production. Marx, and later Marxists, have failed to give these divisions a rigourous theoretical specification.

These notions must be given theoretical substance which removes their cryptic and slogan-like quality. In China, following the Cultural Revolution, the displacement of managerial forms of organisation (in which workers work at the direction of a managerial agency and do not participate in management) and the dispersal of industry and its combination with agriculture are attempts to develop the conditions of advancement of socialist relations of production. Whilst the existence of managerial direction and other forms of centralised administration, and the national and international centralisation of production and the division of labour, are not necessarily capitalist, equally, they are not *necessary* consequences of socialist relations of production. These forms of organisation may contribute to the retardation of the conditions of political advance towards a more developed form of socialist society.[4] Thus, whilst it may be argued that at the level of the relations of production the Soviet Union is a socialist country, the existence of managerial direction, forms of hierarchical social division of labour and centralised administration may be seen as creating political and economic obstacles to the development and revolutionisation of socialist relations of production. Thus the division between the relations of production *per se*, and the organisation and structure of the labour force and forms of centralisation and organisation of production is a serious question which should be investigated by Marxists. It may play an important role in the theory of socialist mode of production and the analysis of the conditions of development of advanced forms of socialism.

B IDEOLOGICAL STATE APPARATUSES

Althusser rejects the legal *form* of the state as the basis for the analysis of state apparatuses. The state/civil society distinction is created by forms of state law and the state, Althusser argues, following Gramsci, is 'above the law' (ISAs, pp. 137–8). The state is defined by its function, the representation and defence of class society. The ideological state apparatuses are identified as *state* apparatuses by their function; the reproduction of the relations of production. They are unified, despite their apparent and necessary diversity, by this function and by the fact that they all represent ruling-class ideology. The unity of the ISAs is therefore the unity of their function and of the foundation of their function, ruling-class ideology and the ruling class. The state in Althusser's analysis can therefore be considered as unified by the function of maintenance of class society. All state apparatuses are ultimately unified by the political and ideological dominance of the ruling class; it is the ruling class which holds and exercises state power.

Althusser questions the unity of the *form* of the state, but he accepts its unity of function. It should be noted here that whilst the state/civil society distinction is indeed effected through state apparatuses, this does not mean that it is not without effects and that it is not, for example in capitalist social formations, a necessary distinction. Legal forms are not illusions without effectivity. Althusser's acceptance of the unity of function can be most clearly seen in the following quotation:

If the ideological state apparatuses 'function' massively and predominantly by ideology, what unifies their diversity is precisely this functioning, in so far as the ideology by which they function is always in fact unified, despite its diversity and contradiction, *beneath the ruling ideology*, which is the ideology of 'the ruling class'. (ISAs, p. 139)

and

The unity of the different ISAs is secured, usually in contradictory forms, by the ruling ideology, the ideology of the ruling class (ISAs, p. 142).

The ideological state apparatuses are *state* apparatuses because of their function and are unified as state apparatuses by the means of performance of that function, ruling-class ideology. The unity of the ideological apparatuses lies outside of them, in the ideological unity of the ruling class. This unity in turn lies outside of it, in the unity of that class *as a class*. Althusser is driven back into the classic problematic of representation. The unity of the ruling class is derived from its economic position and the interests arising from it, as is its position of political dominance. This entails the position that classes, as social forces, exist independently of their representation by the political and ideological instances. It is this existence at the level of the economic which determines the form of their political and ideological representation. Althusser makes this clear: 'the class struggle extends beyond the ISAs because it is rooted elsewhere than in ideology, in the infrastructure, in the relations of production . . .' (ISAs, p. 140). Althusser explicitly adopts the social topography of Marx's *1859 Preface*. Classes as social forces are directly constituted by the economic structure, their 'interests' are given independently of ideological and political practice and their political and ideological representatives are directy determined by the economic. Classes as social forces exist prior to and independently of representation and determine it. This priority reflects, in the *1859 Preface*, a tendency towards vulgar materialism, it involves the base-superstructure contestation. It is in effect the challenge of the idealist philosophy of history, a challenge which involves the assertion of the primacy of matter.

If we consider either the capitalist or the socialist systems, it will be clear that this notion of the givenness of the classes as social forces in the structure of the economic is problematic. It entails an economistic concept of the economy, that is, an economy which generates and determines its own conditions of existence. Classes in capitalist relations of production, capital and wage labour, are 'generalities' which do not correspond to the classes as social forces represented in capitalist social formations in politics and ideology. There is no such thing as a 'working class' (that is a class equivalent to all wage labourers) as a social force in capitalism; nor, indeed, is there a political ideological or economic homogeneity of capital. The same may be said to be true of socialist social formations. Classes in socialist social formations involve political policy and ideological social relations as central conditions of existence. We have discussed already the importance and consequences of systems of management and organisation which are not reducible to the relations of production in creating conditions for and obstacles to socialist development. The formation of classes as social forces involves ideological and political determinations. If these determinations are to be more than simply complexifications of a pre-given class unity which they must express, then they must have a definite effect upon classes as social forces. If the ideological and political relations are, as Althusser and others argue, 'relatively autonomous', this relative autonomy must effect a real determination.

If we consider the concept of representation, and regard it as anything other than a complicated form of reflection, then it must entail *means* of representation, which have a definite effect on the represented constituted by them. It is not too much to argue that once any autonomy is conceded to these means of representation, it follows necessarily that the means of representation determine the represented. This obliterates the classical problem of 'representation' and requires a non-reductionist theory of the political and ideological 'levels'. Classes as social forces, as the forces which appear in politics and in, what we shall continue to call for the moment, the 'ideological', are formed and transformed by the conditions of the political representation and its effects, and by ideological social relations.

It is clear here that Althusser retreats back beyond even the complicated economism of the 'relative autonomy of the political' towards a simple and essentially economistic concept of representation. This is not an accident. The concept of the 'relative autonomy of the political' is a fragile one, it attempts to overcome economism without facing the theoretical consequences of doing so. It constantly relapses either into being merely a complex form of economism, or, conceiving the state and the political 'level' as in some way a calculating subject reacting upon the economy.

Althusser's question – how is it that the relations of production are reproduced? – accepts the primacy of the 'economy'. The 'point of view of reproduction' amounts to asking the question, what is necessary for existing class relations to be maintained?

ISAs become agencies of the perpetuation of given class relations. That is, the class relations to be maintained are specified independently of the means of their maintenance. Class society is unaffected by the forms in which its conditions of existence are provided. ISAs become agencies for the realisation of a functional task given by the economy. The theses of the 'relative autonomy of the superstructure' and 'reciprocal action of the base' complicate but do not alter economism. The economy is here conceived as an auto-existent instance with 'needs'. Complexification results from the fact that these needs require agencies other than the economic in order that they may be met. In all this Althusser retains the problem of the primacy of the economy; the relations of production and classes are given in the economic and require only to be maintained by adequate ideological conditioning.

If the ideological state apparatuses do not represent an already existing ruling class, with unified 'interests', what then is the basis of their unity? The unity of the ISAs as we have seen lies outside them in the unity of ruling-class ideology and the unity of the ruling class as a class. Once this given unity of the ruling class as an economic class is denied, then there is no necessary unity to the ISAs and no grounds for their existence as *state* apparatuses. The ISAs are defined by their function and unified by it. They can have no existence unless they are assigned this function by a pre-existent system of classes and class ideologies.

Where does this leave the concept of ideology? Does this deny the existence of the area of ideological social relations, as we may call it, which Althusser has attempted, however inadequately, to explore? Our position is that what we will continue for the moment to call 'ideological' social relations do have effects upon the form of classes as social forces. We use the word 'ideological' to refer to a non-unitary complex of social practices and systems of representations which have political significances and consequences. To reject the sociological interpretation of ideology (reading through the origin) and to deny any pre-given ideological unity to social relations is not to abandon any political and class analysis of 'ideological' forms. 'Class' analysis we may retain, not in the sense of sociological reduction but of political evaluation. Not a reference to the origin, but a consideration of effect. Hence 'ideological' analysis involves the calculation of the political consequences of social relations and representations. This analysis, however, cannot be one 'outside' of politics; what the calculation of effect *is* depends upon one's political position. This means that the analysis of ideology cannot be other than political. Consequences can only be adduced from a definite political position. Hence the political nature of ideology can never be read off from its 'origin' (indeed, the very notion of an origin is an illusion).

This means that no 'ideological' form or social relation is in essence and in principle bourgeois or non-bourgeois. This may seem a surprising conclusion but is an inevitable and necessary one once the problematic of the origin is abandoned. The political analysis of what we will still call 'ideologies' necess-arily entails the construction of conceptions of the forms of socialism and the conditions of socialist practice by means of which the role of social relations and representation and their consequences may be calculated. This means that ideologies which are, for example, considered 'bourgeois' because they are articulated by managers might be of the first importance for socialism.

It would seem clear that ideological social relations in this sense exhibit no necessary unity of origin or function. Further the political status and consequences of ideological social relations may change with changing social and political conditions, and with the change and development in socialist ideology. Hence any assessment of an ideology or of ideological social relations is not forever always given because it has been made. Hence the social 'origin' of ideologies is no proof of their political status. Ideologies which are advanced by manual workers are not therefore necessarily progressive. Whether they be considered 'implanted', or arising 'spontaneously', they *may* be considered reactionary.

It will be seen, therefore, that the evaluation of ideologies (that is, the *political* analysis of social relations and representations) always entails political calculation and always takes place from the standpoint of a political position. Those who conceive the present conjuncture for example to be a 'revolutionary situation' will calculate very differently from those who believe the prospects for the advance of socialist politics (let alone anything else) are bleak. This will be reflected across the board in issues as diverse as incomes policy or Women's Liberation. Let us take the latter example. Clearly, if one conceives the struggle for socialism as a prolonged one, and if one considers that there exists a diverse complex of social relations not bound by economically given class positions but which have an effect on the representation and formation of classes as social forces, then one will evaluate the question of Women's Liberation quite differently from someone who believes that we are at present in a revolutionarysituation and that class interests are immediately given at the level of the economic. It is politically important to argue that socially created sexual differences are not simply effects of economic relations and will not simply disappear through changes in relations at the level of the economy. This is not to argue that they are not without economic and political effects. The destruction of the forms of political and cultural backwardness and non-participation in which women are enmeshed cannot be other than politically progressive, cannot than other destroy one of the major bastions of reactionary politics in Britain and Europe. However, it should not be supposed that these forms of subordination can be transformed simply by reforms or by ideological struggle campaigns. In so far as they do not depend on the economy in any simple sense and have a complex psychic dimension, the significance of which we hardly yet understand, then there can be no immediate end or revolutionary transformation of this position. The realisation of this fact will not weaken the ideological struggle for Women's Liberation but will develop it and extend it, for it will be realised that there is no simple solution or programme.

Marxists must get used to the idea that important social divisions are not simply dependent on particular forms of the economy and politics and that they will not vanish with their supercession. Men and women, mental and manual labour, town and country, have vital social and political consequences. They will only be transformed by practices which engage their specificity and recognise its political significance. The persistent sociologism and economism of Marxism has become an obstacle to this. This is a field of struggle in which Marxists find themelves ill-equipped. Despite the fact that he has posed the questions in a way which we find unacceptable, Althusser has attempted to raise the problem and to conceive what he calls 'ideological' social relations as a specific level of political problems. This is an intervention of the first importance upon whose mistakes we are dependent for any advances we make.

C   THE MECHANISM OF IDEOLOGY

We have seen that Althusser conceives ideology as a representation of men's 'lived relation' to their conditions of existence and that this relation is an 'imaginary' one. This thesis is a result of the contestation of humanism/historicism: in displacing the constitutive subject Althusser must also displace the classical conception of ideology as a false recognition of the real. Reality can be known in experience only if it exists in a form adequate to experience, that is, as the immediate or alienated product of the subjects who recognise or mis-recognise it. Althusser displaces the notion of the constitutive subject but not the concept of subject: the concept of an 'imaginary' relation supposes a subject who 'lives' that relation. The 'imaginary' is a concept which supposes recognition; it is both an *image* (object or recognition) and a spectral reality (it is only itself, it 'reflects' nothing but itself). The 'imaginary' is not the *imagination* of the subject; as if the subject were prior to the 'imaginary', imagination being an action of the subject. The subject exists through the imaginary relation – in recognition it becomes a subject. It is the recognition in the 'imaginary', in the mirror form of the Other which (to use Althusser's phrase) 'interpellates individuals as subjects'.

The 'imaginary' relation forms the subjects who 'live' it. The subject is formed in the mechanism of ideology through the recognition of an imaginary Subject which 'hails' its recognisor, recognising him *as a subject* and thereby giving recognition by the subject the effect of subjectivity. All ideology entails the Subject as a pole of the 'imaginary' relation. The structure of ideology is 'speculary' (ISAs p. 168), thus the subject exists in the mirror of the Subject/Other, it becomes a subject in its recognition/ reflection of/in the Other, and the Subject exists only in its recognition by subjects (in its effects). Subject and subject reflect one another in a dual mirror relation. The subject is constituted in this speculary relation, it is an effect, but the effect of that effect is that the subject recognises itself as *constitutive*, as an essential subject in a free relation or dialogue with the Subject. Subjects 'work by themselves', that is 'as if' they were constitutive. They 'obey' the commands of the Other as 'free' choices: 'the individual is interpellated as a (free) subject in order that he shall submit freely to the commandments of the subject, i.e. in order that he shall (freely) accept his subjection' (ISAs, p. 169).

Althusser treats the subject not as an essence but as an effect: the subject is constituted but in a mode such that it conceives itself as constitutive. Althusser 'saves the phenomena' of the classic philosophical concept of subject (and retains certain of its central concepts – 'subject, consciousness, belief, actions' ISAs, p. 159) but denies any essential ontological unity to these phenomena. Rejecting the humanist hypostatization of the subject he does not deny that the forms of subjectivity have effects. Althusser argues (retaining a term he has shown to be problematic) that the 'real overdetermines the imaginary', that is, that forms of the imaginary relation correspond to definite structures of social relations (the 'place' of the imaginary is not the same in capitalism as it is, say, in feudalism, nor, therefore, are its forms), and, that the 'imaginary overdetermines are real', that is, that the practices of subjects which are operative through ideology have effects on the totality of social relations.

There can be no doubt that Althusser makes brilliant use of the materials to hand, Lacan's concept of the 'mirror phase'[5] and forms taken primarily from Christian religious ideology. The concept of the constituted/constitutive subject is a masterly means of retaining the forms of subjectivity whilst rejecting humanist explanations of social relations. Althusser's 'mechanism' saves the subject for its own theoretical purposes but it fails to problematise and repose the notion of 'subject' in such a way that it could lead to further theoretical work. There are a number of serious problems with Althusser's conception of the mechanism of ideology:

(i) The analysis of the dual-mirror relation is converted into theory of the genesis of concrete individuals (not-yet-subjects) into social subjects. This follows from the function assigned to ideology in the text:

> 'So be it! . . .' This phrase which registers the effect to be obtained proves that it is no 'naturally' so. . . . This phrase proves that it *has* to be so if things are to be what they must be . . . : if the reproduction of the relations of production is to be assured . . . every day, in the 'consciousness', i.e. in the attitudes of individual-subjects occupying the posts which the socio-technical division of labour assigns to them . . .(ISAs, p. 170)

We shall discuss in greater detail (and at the price of some repetition) below the consequences of this theory of genesis, that it involves a 'circle' – that the subject is pre-supposed as a condition the functioning of its mechanism of formation.

(ii) Althusser fails to answer the central question posed by his theory of ideology:

> 'why is the representation given to individuals of their (individual) relation to the social relations which govern their conditions of existence and their collective and individual life necessarily an imaginary relation' (ISAs, p. 155).

This question amounts to the following, can subjects exist only in the relation of the 'imaginary'? Can one retain the notion of a constituted subject which has no essence without retaining Althusser's concept of the 'imaginary'?

Althusser's concept of subject supposes that subjects and individuals correspond; that the subject is the unitary 'identity' of the individual, that the subject effect corresponds to the classic philosophical conception of 'consciousness'. This is to retain the classic concept whilst bracketing certain of its ontological implications. It is possible, however, to conceive the human individual not as the unitary terminal of an 'imaginary' subject, but as the support of a decentred complex of practices and statuses which have distinct conditions of existence. Two questions are at stake here: the first is the conception of the human individual as a unity of 'consciousness'; the second is the question of whether the only 'subjects' are those which are 'interpellated' individuals? This involves two other questions: (a) What is the form of unity of the subject, is it the 'experience' of 'consciousness', and (b) Is there a form of relation of subjects to their practices and conditions other than the recognition of the 'imaginary'?

Althusser treats the problem of the subject and the 'imaginary' relation as equivalents; subjects exist in the 'imaginary'. There is a further equation at stake here, as we have seen, the identification of the subject and the human subject. Althusser in rejecting humanism/historicism challenges the notion of the constitutive subject and rejects the notion of collective subjects (classes, etc.) found in certain forms of 'Hegelian' Marxism. This rejection of the collective/constitutive subject further reinforces the identification of the subject and the individual.

There are at least two modes of posing the concept of 'subject' as a problem which lead to conclusions quite different from Althusser's and do not fall under his strictures against humanism and historicism.

The first concerns the theory of the psyche. Althusser's subject is conceived at the level of 'conscious' functioning in the psychic structure. The 'conscious' is, however, but one level of the decentred totality of the psyche. The 'concrete individual' (psychic totality) is ec-centric, reducible to no principle of unity. 'Conscious' thought may *represent* itself as a unity coincident with the individual, but the 'concrete individual' (in Althusser's sense) is *not* a subject. Rather, this 'individual' is the effect of the totality of psychic processes (of which the 'conscious' is but one form of determination); these processes cannot be reduced to 'subjectivity'. Althusser's 'concrete individual'/'concrete subject' (is despite the Lacanian analogy) a being prior to psycho-analysis. It represents that philosophical conception of the unity of the 'conscious' which Freud so effectively displaced in his 1915 paper 'The Unconscious'.

The second concerns theories of 'subjects' as the supports of processes. There are two basic conceptions of 'subject' here (which are not contradictory), the juridical and what (for want of anything better) we will call the operational. The juridical conception refers to the designation by legal/customary/political forms of entities which function as supports of processes or as agents in them. The simplest example here is the concept of legal subject. Legal subjects are entities created through legal recognition which are capable (in the forms of law) of initiating actions (suits, pleas, etc.) and of supporting certain statuses (possession, responsibility, etc.). Such subjects exist only relative to legal recognition (they cannot exist in law otherwise, other entities are represented only as possessions of subjects or objects of dispute between them). Legal recognition confers unity on non-human entities (joint-stock companies, public bodies, trusts, etc.) and may deny the status of subject to human individuals (to slaves, subordinates, etc.[6]). To be denied the status of a legal subject is not inconsequential, it is to be unable to initiate legal actions or to support the consequences of actions (thus a dog may own property through a trust and have rights that a bankrupt does not). Civil rights and political representation may be conceived in a similar way. The 'operational' conception of the subject refers to agencies that have an effectivity on the process (whatever it may be) in which they are involved and where one of the determinants of that effect is the 'calculation' the agency undertakes as a condition of its operation. That is, there is no automatic effect of the agent, a condition of effect is that it calculates its relation to the process according to some definite means of calculation. To relieve these abstraction we will use the familiar notion of economic calculation and conceive the agency as a producer of commodities. We know that such agencies need not take the form of human subjects; joint-stock companies are an obvious example. To say that such companies are supported by human subjects (directors, functionaries, etc.) is to ignore the fact that the support cannot take the place of what it supports without a change in its status and effect – corporate forms of possession of the means of production involve legal and economic capacities which human subjects (on a social scale) cannot have. Further, the 'supports' serve relative to the economic units' relation to the processes of production and circulation, they use objective means of calculation (not subjective faculties) to assess the *economic subject*'s relation to these processes, and their own relation to these processes only exists as a condition of the subject's relation.

Whether we use juridical or 'operational' categories, the subjects involved cannot be conceived in terms of an 'imaginary' relation. They are not consciousnesses but they are subjects, nevertheless. Subjects in the sense of *agents*. These subjects may confront human individuals also recognised as subjects in the processes in which both function as agents. Thus an industrial capitalist corporation may compete with an independent artisan producer in the same commodity market. The parents of a deformed child may sue a drug company, or, a man may take the dog who has employed him (through a trust) to an industrial tribunal for unfair dismissal.

If these non-human subjects are not inscribed in the 'imaginary' then there is no reason to suppose that the forms of calculation which are a necessary element in determining their effects (economic calculation, advocacy, etc.) can be reduced to any 'imaginary' relation. Even if these calculations are supported by human individuals they cannot be reduced to a recognition structure since they are determined by conditions which have no necessary correspondence to an 'imaginary' relation.

(iii) Althusser's conception of the function of ideology restores its classic status as a false representation which serves to perpetuate the existing order of things. Despite his opposition to the notion of ideology as 'false consciousness' Althusser's conception of ideology involves *méconnaissance* as its main (and functional) effect:

> The reality in question in this mechanism, the reality which is necessarily *ignored* (*méconnue*) in the very forms of recognition (ideology = misrecognition/ignorance) is indeed, in the last resort, the reproduction of the relations of production and of the relations deriving from them. (ISAs, p. 170)

This recognition/misrecognition is known as such only from the effects of scientific knowledge. Nevertheless Althusser requires the *effects* of falsity (maintenance of the existing order) in just the same way as classical theories.

(iv) Althusser separates 'representation' and the 'lived relation' it represents. His analysis of ideology is in effect an analysis of the 'lived relation' and not of representations of it. In the ISAs paper ideology and the 'imaginary' are equivalent. In *For Marx* theoretical ideology was an elaboration and rationalisation of practical-social ideology. What is the status of 'representation' here? Surely the 'imaginary' and its 'representation' (ideology) cannot be separated? Does not Althusser's imaginary consist in representations in the broadest sense of the terms (signs, concepts, etc.)? A number of questions arise from these problems:

(*a*) How are the forms in the 'imaginary' relation generated? The Subject, his 'words', the substance of his 'commands' pose the question of their conditions of existence. The *forms* of the 'imaginary' cannot arise spontaneously from the subject (that would convert recognition into *imagination* and restore the constitutive subject), equally, they cannot be given by 'reality' (that would restore a simple reflection theory). The forms of the 'imaginary' should, if these positions were to be avoided, have the status of *significations*, representations which are reducible neither to a represented which is beyond them, nor to an origin in a subject, but which are effects of the action of means of representation. Such a conception makes the very notion of 'representation' problematic. This raises the question of the determinants of those means, of their signifying action, and of the relation of the subject to them. These questions challenge the functional necessity of the effects of the 'imaginary'.

(*b*) What is the reason why a particular set of means of representation dominate so as to create the particular spectacles of the 'imaginary'; why is there a single dominant spectacle and so a single interpellation?

Posing these questions is to take Althusser into a region where his theory has no answers. The recognition structure for all its subtlety, simply supposes that the spectacle exists and this it is recognised, once we move outside of this sensationalist theatre, once we question the places its actors occupy, there are no answers. We shall see, in discussing the genesis of the subject-individual, that this mechanism is nothing but an elaborate metaphor, using the forms of the subject-object structure of knowledge in classical philosophy. It presupposes the subject, but it also takes the object of recognition as a given – it has no account of the existence of the forms of the 'imaginary' except a functionalism.

We shall now consider separately and in more detail the questions raised by Althusser's analysis of the genesis of subjectivity in 'concrete individuals' and the concept of 'representation'.

D   THE GENESIS OF THE SUBJECT INDIVIDUAL

The nature of the mechanism of ideology corresponds to the social function ideology is assigned to perform in the ISAs paper. The questions Althusser poses in respect of this mechanism are constituted in relation to this function. How are concrete individuals formed as subjects? By what means do they function as subjects who 'live' class oppression and exploitation as 'necessity' and accept them? As we have seen, he explains both questions by the dual mirror-relation structure which characterises all ideological recognition. In the dual mirror relation a homogeneous space of reflection is established between the subject (s) and the master subject (S). In the relation s→S, the subject recognises himself as a subject in the mirror of the Subject; in the otherness which becomes his own reflection. In the relation S→s, the subject is merely the mirror form or image of the Subject; his spectral quality as a phenomenon of ideology makes possible his identity and his reflection. A space of perpetual reflection is established; a space purely internal to ideology.

Althusser maintains the internality of this space by distinguishing between the subject and the concrete individual. This difference conceals the sensationalist theoretical forms which the mechanism requires in order to perform the task of interpellation. The dual-mirror relation only works if the subject (s) who recognises already has the attributes of a knowing subject; the mirror of the Subject serves as a means of reflection, giving the subject an *image*, that image is, however, *recognised* by the subject as *its* image. Recognition, the crucial moment of the constitution (activation) of the subject, presupposes a point of cognition prior to the recognition. Something must recognise that which it is to be. The space of the dual mirror relation is only possible on the condition that it ever already exists and that it concerns nothing outside it (i.e. nothing which does not already posses the capacities to be inside it). But this space must necessarily have dealings with the 'exterior', if ideology is to generate its social effects. The social function of ideology is to constitute concrete indivíduals (not-yet-subjects) as subjects. The concrete individual is 'abstract', it is not yet the subject it will be. It is, however, *already* a subject in the sense of the subject which supports the process of recognition. Thus something which is not a subject must already have the faculties necessary to support the *recognition* which will constitute it as a subject. It must have a *cognitive* capacity as a prior condition of its place in the process of recognition. Hence the necessity of the distinction of the concrete individual and the concrete subject, a distinction in which the faculties of the latter are supposed already in the former (unless of course cognition be considered a 'natural' human faculty).

Althusser recognises the problematicity of the separation individual-subject:

This is a proposition which entails that we distinguish for the moment between concrete individuals on the one hand and concrete subjects on the other, although at this level concrete subjects only exist insofar as they are supported by a concrete individual. (ISAs, p. 162)

He takes this distinction to be a mere device, a matter of exposition, whereas it is a necessary support of and condition of the whole theory. Here again a necessary consequence of the questions asked is taken to be a mere level of 'abstration' in discourse. The social function of ideology can only operate if the two are distinct, if the concrete individual is constituted as a subject, and the recognition moment of the mechanism can only operate if the individual to be interpellated as a subject already has certain attributes of subjectivity. Later on, Althusser recognises that the dual-mirror relation itself cannot work if the individual is prior to it, outside of it, and not already possessed of the attributes of a subject:

> *Individuals are always-already subjects*. Hence are 'abstract' with respect to the subjects which they always-already are (ISAs, p. 164)

This proposition might seem paradoxical. Individuals are always-already subjects: if this means that they are subjects in the strict sense then they have always existed in ideology and they can be only *ideological* and not *concrete* individuals. Althusser avoids this impasse by placing concrete individuals once more outside ideology but in a new way:

> That an individual is always-already a subject, even before he is born, is nevertheless the plain reality, accessible to everyone and not a paradox at all. Freud shows that individuals are always 'abstract' with respect to the subjects they always-already are, simply by noting the ideological ritual that surrounds the expectation of a 'birth', that 'happy event . . .' Before its birth, the child is therefore always-already a subject . . .(ISAs, pp. 164–5)

Individuals are abstract to the subjects they soon will be and which pre-exist them – the concrete individual, the infant, is *actually* outside the ideological subject prefabricated to receive him by already existing subjects. Thus the constitution of the subject becomes its prefabrication and its projection into a pre-social being. But the complex and hazardous process of formation of a human adult from 'a small animal' does not necessarily correspond to Althusser's mechanism of ideology (the dual-mirror relation) unless the child (and the man) remain in Lacan's mirror-phase, or unless we fill the child's cradle with anthropological assumptions (i.e. we invest the child with the capacity for *cognition* that is necessary for recognition). I have no quarrel with children, I do not wish to pronounce them blind, deaf or dumb, merely to deny that they possess the capacities of *philosophical* subjects, that they have the attributes of 'knowing' subjects independent of their formation and training as social beings. Althusser does not 'believe' this either, but he is committed to the presence of attributes of subjectivity in the subject-to-be by the terms of his theoretical problematic. Althusser is forced to propose the dual-mirror structure as the mechanism of genesis of social subjects from concrete human animals. The subject is internal to the speculary structure, he is presupposed as a subject inside it. Althusser must use this structure to explain the formation of conditioned social subjects, to do so he must suppose elements of subjectivity prior to the mechanism itself. The subject is doubly given.

Althusser's dual-mirror relation supposes either a purely ideological space (a space forever empty of concrete individuals) or a 'subject' prior to ideology. Althusser is in a circle not unlike that of Descartes' Cogito, either he must abandon the substance of his 'problem' or he faces an infinite regress, at each stage of the process encountering the subject he presupposed at the beginning. Just as Descartes' 'I' must ever recede before a rigorous scepticism and yet, within the terms of the problematic, ever remain, so the 'individual', who is prior to ideology and whose pre-ideological attributes of subjectivity are necessary to its becoming a subject, cannot be erased in Althusser's text and must reappear in it. The similarity of these circles is no accident. Althusser's analysis of the 'mechanism' of ideology describes and reproduces certain of the forms of religious and philosophical theory. Further evidence for this is to be found in the fact that the interpellation relation subject-individual can be placed within Althusser's own empiricism–idealism structure of the subject and the essence without undue violence. The subject which the individual is to be represents the essence, an essence which transcends the 'abstract' individual, and the abstract individual represents the 'subject', an empty individual with nothing but the faculties necessary to receivce the subject that it will be. The empiricism of the 'subject' here requires the support of certain prior suppositions (that it is a cognising subject). This idealism of the essence – empiricism of the subject structure does not concern an anthropology – the subject and its predicates are not linked by an anthropological necessity. But it is *only* the the absence of manifest humanist positions, of constitutivity, which demarcates this structure from what Althusser calls the empiricism-idealism couple of philosophical anthropology.

E 'REPRESENTATION'

Althusser conceives ideology in terms of the concept of representation. We have questioned both the economistic conception of the representation of social classes and the conception of ideology as a representation of the 'imaginary' relation. The same concept is at stake in both cases. This concept of 'representation' involves a similar instability to the concept of the 'relative autonomy of the political level'. This instability in both cases concerns the status of the 'represented'. Two distinct positions on the nature of the represented are possible:

(i) that the represented exists outside of the process of representation, that process expresses or reflects it (with a greater or lesser degree of distortion due to the means of representation employed);

(ii) that the represented exists as an effect of a process of signification, it has no existence beyond the process which represents it (it is not an origin to which we may return to question the truth of the reflection).

If what is represented is argued to exist independently of the process of its representation then two consequences follow: either, the represented must determine the process of its representation, reflection being its form of appearance/existence, or, it must exist in a form against which its reflections or expressions may be measured as more or less accurate representations of it (if the represented does not determine the process of representations and if, on the other hand, there is no means of assessing the accuracy of the process then the whole problematic of representation is shattered – the auto- existence of the 'represented' becomes unknowable and has no determinate relation to the process). This division of forms of conception of the represented as an entity independent of the process of representation is overlain by another, that of appearance and essence and of the related forms of cognition of these forms, experience and esoteric knowledge. This division complexifies the former, cross-cutting its poles. The essence of the real may represent itself in the form of appearance. The status of appearance (as representation/ distortion of the essence) is determined by esoteric knowledge which penetrates beyond experience to apprehend the essence. Knowledge of the essence then serves as a measure against which the forms of representation are known as 'appearance' (as the inessential).

'Representation' is a category which entails the classic subject/ object structure of knowledge. The 'represented' (object) exists as the source or measure of its representations. The subject (whether through experience or esoteric knowledge) recognises the represented in or through its representations. The representation becomes an *image* of the represented, a reflection of the object (motivated by or measured against the object). The represented either, determines the conditions of representability – giving representation the form of its expression – or the represented exists in a form auto-accessible to recognition (without representation) as the measure of its forms of expression. This structure is in Althusser's own terms necessarily empiricist. It installs the structure of the essential and the inessential, of knowledge as the recognition of given objects. Reality becomes intelligible in nature: the recognition of its essence is the knowledge of the presence-to-itself of truth. The subject who knows through recognition either, internalises an auto-intelligible reality, or, recognises itself (looses itself) in the externalised form of its own products. The auto-intelligible object (which can be known on sight) depends for its existence-as-intelligibility on a subject which is its origin. On the one hand, this has been accomplished by making reality in essence 'spiritual'; a Logos, at once word and existence, is its origin and essence. The subjects who recognise this intelligible reality/form of appearance are products of the Subject-Logos, moments of recognition internal to the totality of its creation. On the other hand, knowledge can be conceived as the self-recognition of the subject, knowing itself reflected in its own products (illusion is the alienation of the subject to itself) Modern empiricism has saved itself from the Subject (theological foundations of knowledge) by refusing to question the places of this space, refusing to account for the knowing subject or the object known, refusing to explain the possibility of knowledge through experience. Experience has become absolute, a given point of departure and its own guarantee.

Althusser has retained a concept, 'representation', which entails theoretical forms he has shown to be untenable within Marxist discourse (they are tenable only through a rigorous theology, through the dogmatism of 'experience' or (its mirror equivalent) a determined scepticism). The retention of this concept can be accounted for in terms of the problem of 'ideology' Althusser investigates. Althusser seeks to explain certain effects (which involve 'representations') as necessary effects, necessary to certain social relations. It follows that he uses the conception of 'representation' rather than that of signification; the products of signifying practices do not 'represent' anything outside them, they cannot serve as a means of expression of class interests or of (functional) mis-recognition of social relations. We have seen that the concept of the ISAs depends for its role and unity on the representation of class 'interests' formed at the economic level. Equally, ideology 'represents' an 'imaginary' relation of men to their conditions of existence. This relation has a definite functionally necessary form, it must be 'represented' in ideology rather than constituted through practices of signification. The action of such practices cannot be terminated according to the (non-significatory) necessities of a social order. We have seen that Althusser avoids a 'reflection' theory of ideological representation only by a series of refusals and inconsistencies.

The concept of 'representation' entails the possibility that the 'represented' determines its means of representation and the action of those means. Only in this way is it possible for there to be a necessary correspondence (representation-effect) between a 'representation' and what motivates it (the represented). If any autonomy is accorded to the *action* of the means then the relation between them and their product cannot be given (this recalls the problems of the 'relative autonomy' of political representation). If this action is determined then the means cease to be effectivities and become *effects* pure and simple: representation becomes reflection, the means and the image formed by them being one determined whole. 'Ideology' becomes an image whose form is externally given: it can be neither a discourse nor a practice but a form of recognition.

Althusser's difference from the simple reflection ('representation') theories of ideology consists as we have seen in inserting the 'imaginary' relation between the real and ideological representation, and in refusing to give a rigorous account of the status of the forms involved in the 'imaginary' relation and their relation to ideological representation. This *refusal* saves him from the effects of the instability of the concept of representation, he avoids falling into a reflection theory of ideology. Equally, in failing to *displace* this concept he is able to save the questions he asks of ideology but at the price of being unable to deal with the specificity of 'ideological' social relations.

In *Reading Capital* Althusser did provide an account of the imaginary relation (one he refuses in the paper on ISAs because of his rejection of 'Spinozism'). In this earlier text the 'imaginary relation' was an effect of the structure. The structure of a mode of production producing forms of relation of the subject/supports to the process and to one another such that the mode 'functions *as a society*'(*RC* p. 66). This 'society effect' is the effect of the 'imaginary relation'. In the ISAs paper Althusser avoids this ultra-structuralist explanation in which the structure generates its own conditions of existence (we have seen the price this refusal in the postscript imposes on him). In consequence the function-alism of the ISAs paper is weakened by not being made necessary, a function is postulated and agencies assigned to support it, and that is all. This functionalism is not, however, thereby overcome. To develop the position of *Reading Capital* would have entailed making the 'imaginary' an appearance form necessary to the functioning of the structure, providing the subjects/supports it creates with their relation to its existence as process. The recognition effect of the subjects is guaranteed because of the origin of all its elements in the structure. The structure becomes the Subject-Origin of the relation of re-cognition; the Subject which makes possible the 'society effect'. This theological necessitation of the 'imaginary' is avoided, but only by refusals and inconsistencies.

The consequence of rejecting the concept of 'representation' is to destroy the classic Marxist problem of ideology. Althusser's advances had already rendered this concept problematic. This problem requires that there be a correspondence (the latter determines the former) and a non-correspondence (the former misrepresents the latter) between ideology and the reality it represents. If there is any determining action of the means of representation in constituting what is 'represented' by them then these forms of correspondence/non-correspondence are shat-tered. Even if it is argued that the *means* have conditions of existence (the forms of these means 'correspond' to certain forms of social relations, e.g. 'mass' communications require a definite level of technique) it does not follow that the *action* of those means is thereby determined. There is no necessary relation between the conditions of existence of the means of representation and what is produced by the action of those means, no necessity that they 'represent' those conditions.

If what we have hitherto called representations are the product of a practice of signification then there can be no necessary unity to the 'ideological'. Signification abolishes the bounding of this realm by social relations which 'motivate' their (distorted) expression in it; its action is not inscribed in limits set by what it signifies, the signified does not exist prior to its signification. This conception generates a new set of questions, different from the classic sociologistic problems of the theory of ideology (which class do these forms 'represent'?, etc.):

(i) as we have argued the *consequences* of social practices and 'ideologies', what is signified in them, is the form of political or 'class' analysis – this analysis is a form of political calculation/ struggle and depends on a constructed political position;

(ii) how necessary are these consequences as a function of the *means* of signification employed, is it possible that other forms of practice and therefore of action of these means would lead to forms with different consequences? (Thus, for example, do 'mass communications' media necessarily have certain political effects – depoliticisastion, trivialisation – as various 'cultural critics' would claim?)

(iii) the determinants and conditions of existence of these means?

(iv) the determinants and conditions of existence of the practices entailed in their action?

These questions are cryptic in the extreme; they represent nothing like the level of elaboration of Althusser's own answers to the questions he asked. They are intended to indicate the sorts of problems which arise once a reductionist analysis of ideology is abandoned. It is only by abandoning reductionism and the forms of unity that it imposes that we can begin to approach 'ideological' social relations with questions appropriate to their specificity.

NOTES

1. The key texts in this respect are 'Marxism and Humanism' (*Fo Marx*) and 'Freud and Lacan' and 'Ideology and Ideological State Apparatuses' (*Lenin & Philosophy*). Althusser's position on ideology in *Reading Capital* is considered briefly here (section E.). For a discussion of Rancière's position on ideology in *Reading Capital* see Chapter 4.
2. Chapter 2.
3. For a critique of the possibility of such a theory see Hindess and Hirst, Chapter 6.
4. Charles Bettleheim has attempted to stress the role of the divisions of mental and manual labour and town and country as obstacles to be superseded in the development of socialist relations of production. In his text on industrial organisation in China (1974) Bettelheim stresses the importance of the destruction of managerial forms of administration and of the geographical centralisation of industry and culture. These forms he shows are not automatically displaced by a change in the forms of possession or appropriation of the surplus product. They will persist in the absence of practices directed to their supersession. They are consequences of forms of administration and calculation which are not confined to capitalism but, arguably, until the Cultural Revolution were dominant in all the countries attempting (with various results) to construct socialism. For a critical discussion of Bettelheim see Hindess (1976).
5. See Lacan (1968).
6. See Hindess and Hirst (1975) Chapter 3 for a discussion of the legal status of slaves.

4 Rancière, Ideology and Capital

PREFATORY REMARKS

This essay was written in 1972 for the magazine *Theoretical Practice*. Originally it was to have been part of a general theoretical account of the relations between the economic and ideological instances in the different modes of production. This project was conceived in a 'structuralist' manner and was rendered obsolete by the implications of the criticisms of Rancière's and Althusser's theories of ideology which were to have been part of it. The text printed here omits certain portions of the original essay. In the original draft there was a long discussion of the conditions which a theory of ideology must meet. These can be summarised as follows:

(i) That ideology must be conceived as a practice and as the product of a practice. This condition developed Althusser's concept of 'instances' as the levels of articulation of a particular practice into the social totality of practices ('practice' was defined as the transformation of a definite raw material by the determinative action of definite means of production).

(ii) That ideology consisted in signs and representations; these were conceived after Jakobson – as characterised by the 'sliding of the signifier under the signified' – as having no originary meaning outside the process of signification in objects which that process attempts to represent.

Against these conditions both Rancière's and Althusser's very different theories of ideology were found wanting on several counts.

Also omitted here is an early version of the critique of Althusser's ISAs paper; this was subsequently developed and expanded and appears here as Chapter 3. It should also be noted that when this text was written the concept of 'structural causality' had not been fully criticised; in the original version Rancière was criticised for falling short of the (ideal) concept of structural causality. Later it became clear that the notion of structural causality was little different from the 'Hegelian' forms of action of the totality criticised by Althusser in *Reading Capital* (fetishism); Althusser's totality also secured its conditions of existence in its action and produced a realm of necessary effects. This criticism is developed in Chapter 3.

A   IDEOLOGY AS A 'STRUCTURE EFFECT'

Rancière's text, 'The Concept of "Critique" and the "Critique of Political Economy"' contains, although this is not its primary object, a theory of 'ideology'. This theory conceives ideology as an effect accompanying the form of structuration of the economic instance. This conception rests on the following positions:

1. That ideology is not the product of a practice, it is the function of a space created by the structuration of the economic; the absence of the cause in its effects, and the necessary distance between the 'visible' effects and their determinations.
2. The existence of ideology as a function of this space presupposes a subject. The subject is already given in the structure as the means of recognition. This necessary subject who 'sees' the 'visible' effects is located in a structural place, as the subjectivity of this place. The capitalist, occupying this place or location in the structure, will *experience* the appearances which are for him given perceivable facts in *this* way. The structure-effect therefore stages a confrontation between the subject (the subjectivity of the place) and an object (the appearance of the visible

effects of the structure as given facts to the subject). This object and this subject are brought together by two conditions.

(*a*) First, that it is not just any subject, but *this* subject located in *this* place which confronts the given in this way: the places the agents occupy are therefore accorded necessary subjectivities – as capitalist, as worker, etc. The economy can therefore 'work by itself'; it engenders within itself all the capacities of the subjects which are necessary to put it into motion. The effect of this condition is an *economistic* conception of the economy.

(*b*) Second, that the subject and the object are linked by the operation of the concept of *experience*. Any individual so placed, e.g. placed as a capitalist, would 'see things in this way'. The operation of this concept also has two theoretical conditions: (i) that the real be conceived as engendering significations in and of itself, that knowledge is secreted in it to be known in being seen (even if it is the illusory knowledge of experience), and that categories and concepts (the elementary categories which describe the 'surface' of economic phenomena, profit, interest, etc.) are present in the real; (ii) that the subject be conceived within the empiricism/idealism couple structure, that is, as a *rational* subject, at once a being of reason, whose essence is reason, and at the same time an empty being whose reasonableness consists in being able to receive and to be what it is that it receives. The effect of this latter condition is a dual *empiricism* – the interiorisation of an empiricist knowledge in the structure and the reliance on empiricist categories to explain elements of the structure.

The support of the subjectivity of the place, the rational being who becomes a capitalist through experience, and of the concept of experience is the human subject. This subject and his 'faculties' are unconditionally presupposed, no theoretical basis is given for its presence, no attempt is made to account for the possession of the faculties 'given' this subject by humanist ideology. The structuralism which makes ideology an effect of a structure's structuration, and conceives its supports as places created by the structure, in fact requires a humanism for it to work, for these effects to be 'visible' and for these places to be filled.

The conception of ideology as a structure-effect, as a misre-cognition engendered in the subject by the distance between what is given for him to see and the real order of the structure requires a particular conception of structure – of a structure whose structuration is not that of structural causality. There are two indices of this difference. Firstly, there is a direct relation between the structure and something given externally to it, the human subject; this relation exists because the structure requires the presence of this external element as the support of certain of its functions and effects. In reality the structure's determination is limited by and predicated on something whose existence and action it is unable to account for. Secondly, the order of the structure creates a given appearance. Ideology conceived as a structure-effect requires theoretical conditions which create a 'slide' away from structural causality toward expressive caus-ality; a tendency for the structure and its effects to be disposed toward the poles of an essence-appearance model. The structure and its effects are separated; the structure existing behind and beyond the forms of the given it establishes as their truth and *raison d'être*. The given the structure establishes becomes the inessential, the dross of visible forms in which the essential of the structure hides itself. In the most developed forms of this conception of ideology as a structure-effect the given attains the specificity of a *screen*; it is in no sense equivalent to the effects in which the structure is inscribed, which are the presence and reality of the structure in structural causality.

The registration of the possibility of such humanist and Hegelian conceptual forms, *experience*, *essence-appearance*, the pre-given subject, in a discourse such as that of Rancière's (the actuality of that possibility will be determined in the critique which follows) which is avowedly anti-Hegelian and anti-Humanist should not surprise us. No discourse can be judged by its own claims. But the site of this presence of apparently alien and unexpected conceptual forms is a significant one. Althusser registered the presence of Hegelian concepts, of an Hegelian logic and their theoretical effects at the same point in Marx's *Capital*. This point is the theory of *fetishism*; an ideological structure-effect of the economic. Althusser designates the effect of the absence of a concept of the effectivity of the structure on its elements in *Capital*:

> It will no doubt be said that this is merely a word, and that only the word is missing, since the object of the word is there complete. Certainly, but this word is a *concept*, and the repercussions of the structural lack of this concept can be found in certain precise theoretical effects on certain assignable *forms* of Marx's discourse, and in certain of his identifiable *formulations* which are not without their consequences. Which may help to illuminate, but this time from *within* . . . the real *presence* of certain Hegelian forms and references in the discourse of *Capital*. From *within*, as the exact measurement of the disconcerting but inevitable absence, the absence of the concept (and of all the sub-concepts) of the *effectivity of the structure on its elements* which is the visible/invisible, absent/present keystone of his whole work.
>
> *Reading Capital* (p. 29)

A specific theoretical effect of the presence of Hegelian forms is the mode in which 'fetishism' is thought:

> In his search for a concept with which to think the remarkable reality of the effectivity of a structure on its elements, Marx often slipped into the really almost inevitable use of the *classical* opposition between *essence and phenomenon* . . . But how many of Marx's texts present *fetishism* as an 'appearance', an 'illusion' arising purely in 'consciousness', show us the real, inner movement of a process 'appearing' in a fetishised form of the 'consciousness' of the same subjects in the form of an apparent movement.
>
> *RC* (pp. 190–1)

Althusser links a specific theoretical absence, of the concept of structural causality, with the presence of the conception of ideology as a given structure-effect.

Althusser thus attempted to confine the effects of this lack to a definite region of *Capital*, to the theory of fetishism. Althusser, unlike Rancière, challenges conceptions of the structure as generating 'appearances'. 'Appearence' requires for its existence a given subject of recognition. Althusser's alternative mode of representation of the structure to the agents, 'structural causality', does not reject the notion of *necessary* effects of the whole nor of *méconnaisance* as the condition on which subjects function as supports of the whole. The process of representation remains subject to the logic of the structure. Althusser's significant innovation is to challenge the concept of a given subject and to attempt to replace it by one constituted within the structure. As Chapter 3 shows this attempt fails and a given subject prior to the process is posited just as it is in Rancière and Marx.

B   RANCIÈRE

The primary object of Rancière's text is not the production of a theory of ideology. In order to demarcate the discursive structure of the *1844 Manuscripts* and the 1843 *Critique of Hegel's Philosophy of Right* from the logic of *Capital* Rancière chooses the region of *Capital*, theory of value-commodity form-fetishism. He does so because of the manifest presence of Hegelian terminology and Hegelian theoretical forms (in appearance at least) in these sections of *Capital*. A proof that the logic of *Capital at this point* is not reducible to the logic of *1843/1844* is the strongest and most relevant demonstration of the separation of the two discourses. Rancière challenges the arguments for a continuity between *1844* or *1843* and *Capital* (Della Volpe, Pietranera, etc.) on the ground where they are apparently strongest. He proves that the concepts and theoretical structures of *Capital* cannot be reduced to the terms of the anthropological critique of *1844*: that in *Capital* there is no constitutive subject, and no subject/predicates-objectification/alienation structure. He proves that the model of the speculative discourse of the *1843 Critique* is not the form of the scientific discourse of *Capital*.

The crucial form of demarcation for Rancière is the demonstration that anthropological explanations and radical humanism are absent in *Capital*. In the course of his analysis Rancière presents a theory of ideology in respect of fetishism and other themes: here three specific examples of the presence of this theory will be posed and criticised.

1   *Hypostatisation in the 1843 Critique and Capital*

Rancière argues that the sensuous-supersensuous character of the commodity, as a concrete object with a social usefulness and as a 'bearer' of value, reproduces the moment of *incarnation* (the mystical idea 'sovereignty' is incorporated a particular individual, the monarch) from the hypostatisation structure of the speculative Hegelian discourse criticised in *1843*:

> Here we have come once again upon the concept of the support which we located in the diagram of the anthropological critique of speculation, and with it we return to a function which corresponds to the function of *incarnation* in this same diagram. The empirical thing (the coat) becomes the support for the supernatural abstraction *value* just as the empirical existence of the monarch became the incarnation of the abstract category *sovereignty* in Hegel.
>
> *Theoretical Practice* 2 (p. 38)

Rancière argues that the structures of the two incarnations are *homologous*:

> It is not just because it is a question of . . . [value] . . . here and of sovereignty in the *Manuscript* of 1843 that we can affirm the homology between the structure of incarnation which constituted an element of the general structure of speculation in the text of 1843. Value is incarnated in the empirical

existence of the coat, just as . . . sovereignty is incarnated in the empirical existence of the Hegelian monarch.

TP 2 (p. 38)

The homology Rancière argues is one of *form*, the theoretical function of this identical incarnation form in *Capital* is quite different from that in the 1843 *Critique*. The difference consists in this, that in the 1843 *Critique* hypostatisation-incarnation pertained to the structure of the *speculative discourse* – the incarnation is the sensuous existence of the 'idea', the 'idea' is itself the supersensuous form of another real sensuous existent that has been separated from it by an abstraction – while in *Capital* incarnation is a process which takes place *in the real itself*. This real process is not the abstraction-hypostatisation-incarnation of the attributes of a truly constitutive subject, but a 'speculative' moment of a process without a subject. In *Capital* 'reality is speculative': it is no longer possible to proceed directly from the appearance of things to their essence, for they are separated by the speculative structure of the real itself. *Capital* can no longer sustain the myth which is the foundation of the earlier 'critique', of a reading at sight (of the essence visible in 'its' phenomena). The real is so structured as to present us with a puzzle which cannot be resolved by means of its immediate appearance:

We are no longer concerned with a *text* calling for a reading, which will give its underlying meaning, but with a *hieroglyph* which has to be deciphered. This deciphering is the work of science. The structure which excludes the possibility of critical reading is the structure which opens the dimension of science.

TP 2 (p. 39)

Appearance is not a mere obstacle, a circumstantial phenomenon which hides the esence, it is positively deceptive to an 'ordinary perception' and it leads to conclusions drawn from such perceptions which conceal the real determination of things:

The character of this *Gegenstandlichkeit* is such that it is only recognised for what it is – i.e. as a metonymic manifestation of the structure – in science. In ordinary perception it is taken for a property of the things as such. The social character of the products of labour appears as a natural property of these products as mere things.

TP 2 (p. 37)

It is possible to say, following on the 'homology' of incarnation, that the appearance of the structure in its phenomena is in an alienated mode, the mode of an alienation in which the 'predicates' cannot be restored to the 'subject' except by a new kind of perception.

This 'appearance' is produced by the action of a 'metonymic' causality

Thus the formal operations which characterise the space in which economic objects are related together manifest social processes while concealing them. We are no longer dealing with an anthropological causality referred to the act of a subjectivity, but with a quite new causality which we can call metonymic causality . . . Here we can state it as follows: what determines the connexion between the effects (the relations between commodites) is the cause (the social relations of production) insofar as it is absent.

TP 2 (p. 36)

This causality is non-anthropological because it has no centre and no subject as its centre. The subject does not intervene in 'the constitution of the phenomenon', rather it is the cause whose absence constitutes the sensuous *objects of perception*. These objects which appear as 'givens' to the subject are the effects of a subjectless process. 'Appearance', and its ideological and false character, exists in the separation of the conditions of determination of objects and the conditions in which they are perceived, in the difference between the real determinants and the apparent determinations the subject perceives:

What characterises *appearance* (*Schein*) is the fact that this thing appears in it simply as a sensuous thing and that its properties appear as natural properties.

Thus the constitution of objects does not appertain to a subjectivity. What does appertain to a subjectivity is perception. Appearance (*Schein*) is determined by the gap between the conditions of constitution of the objects and the conditions of their perception.

TP 2 (p. 40)

Rancière, therefore, explicitly states that perceptible phenomena are effects or appearances of a structure, and that a subject which perceives them is supposed in relation to the structure.

Rancière does not register this homology between the 1843 *Critique* and *Capital* as a problem: for him it is sufficient that there is a non-identity of function between the two forms. Thus the substitution of the relationship sensuous/supersensuous-social for the relationship human/sensuous as far as Rancière is concerned transforms the whole theoretical problematic. It does so in the sense that it shifts the terrain from anthropology to anti-humanism. But there is a more extensive 'homology' between the incarnation structures of the *Critique* and *Capital*. The theoretical support of the sensuous/supersensuous couple is the couple subject/object ('given' object-perceiving subject) which plays a vital part in the theory of the fetishism of commodities since it makes their 'fetish' character possible (sensuous – thing/ supersensuous-relation, visibility of thing – invisibility of relation). Hence while the anthropological empiricism of the 1843 *Critique* is not present, the terms of a more general empiricist problematic are common to the *Critique* and Rancière's presentation of the arguments of *Capital*. Rancière's 'fetishism' depends on a causality which actualises an empiricist mode of knowing in the real, which stages a confrontation between a concrete subject and the 'appearance' of concrete objects. For Rancière's fetishism to work empiricist epistemology must be a valid account of a real mode of knowing (even if that mode is an ideological mode) – the process of empiricist knowledge – subject → perception → object → knowledge → subject – must be actually viable.

2 *Real and Apparent Motion*

Here Marx distinguishes between two motions:

> a *real* motion which is the movement of value, a movement which is concealed in the repetition of the process of circulation, and an *apparent* motion, a movement accredited by everyday experience, and which presents the inverse of the real motion.
>
> *Theoretical Practice* 6 (pp. 32–3)

The real motion of the process is *concealed* and the apparent motion *inverts* the real motion. The capitalist process as a whole (production-circulation) inverts its inner determinations and presents a *surface connexion* of things which is the inverse of real or inner connexion. The 'play' (in the mechanical sense) of the real and apparent motions constitutes the ideology-effect which is inherent in the structure of the whole process (which is part of the structure of the structure), the effect which makes the real opaque and establishes the surface of manifest objects given to perception:

> This development ends with the forms which are manifest at the surface of capitalist production, those in which different capitals confront one another in competition, and which are perceived in their daily experience by the economic subjects to whom Marx gives the name of *agents of production*.
>
> *TP* 6 (p. 33)

Only the apparent motion of the process is 'given' to the perception of the 'agents':

> It is the form of apparent motion or of the connection of things

which is given to the perception of the agents of production.
TP 6 (p. 33)

This notion of the real and apparent motions of a process provides the foundation on which three discourses are differentiated: that of *science*, which is the resolution of the visible movement into the intrinsic movement, apparent into real motion; that of the *real* itself, the speculative discourse of concealment-inversion which resolves the real into the apparent motion; and that of *ideology*, the discourse of the subject of the process, the conscious expression of the apparent motion. Science inverts the inversion – it *reverses* the speculative discourse of the real. For the subject confined to his place in the process there can be no other knowledge than ideology; the elaboration of the *results* of the speculative discourse of the real. Science must therefore be a knowledge from a vantage point *beyond* the process, it cannot be the product of any subject of the process. Science's 'conceptual grasp' upon the structure of the whole process is an effect of its recognition of the speculative discourse *from the other side, from the side of the real motion*. Science could therefore be called the conscious expression by a non-subject of the whole process from vantage point of the real motion. It will be noted that the terms real-apparent, inner-outer, surface-depth, manifest-hidden, etc., variations of the essence-appearance form (the form of realisation of the essence in its phenomena in which it is hidden) force science into the conception of a point of view:

> A scientific analysis of competition in fact presupposes an analysis of the inner nature of capital, just as the apparent motions of the heavenly bodies are not intelligible to any but him who is acquainted with their real motions.
> Marx *Capital*, Vol. 1, p. 316: cited by Rancière *TP* 6 (p. 33)

Science and ideology almost become a matter of *perspective*. Thus the knowledge of the subject is limited by its *place*. A subject differently situated, a subject which transcended this place, could doubtless see more of the structure; just as a subject situated on the Sun would see things differently from a subject situated on the Earth. Empiricism, once admitted, can only be limited by its *localisation*, but it is admitted on the basis of a need of the structure for such an empiricism, and its immediate form, localised in the subject, is not the end of its influence. Science becomes conceived in an empiricist mode as a knowledge which *sees* more of the structure, which cognises the whole (essence *and* appearance) rather than a part.

> . . . We can see the outline of a theory of capitalist subjectivity, a theory of motors and motives, completely different from the *1844 Manuscripts*. It is not the motives of the capitalist that turn against him in the form of objectivity; it is the tendencies specific to *capital*, the structural laws of the capitalist mode of production, that, through the phenomena of competition, are internalised as motives by the capitalists.
>
> *TP* 6 (p. 33)

The capitalist subject, an agent of the process, is defined as a personification or embodiment of certain relations of production, its intervention in the process is 'not as a constitutive subject but as a perceiving subject trying to explain to itself the relations it perceives'. (R/3, p. 38). The capitalist, as the decisive subjectivity of the process, learns to play his part by *experience*:

> Experience teaches certain regular connections, for example a connection between wages and the prices of commodities from which can be drawn the conclusion that an increase in wages raises prices.
>
> *TP* 6 (p. 38)

The instruments of this subject's knowledge are *experience* and intuition. The capitalist is a rational being who learns to act in accordance with the nature of the things which it is given to him to perceive. The capitalist internalises as the motives for his action the logic of the phenomena of the apparent motion and this motion's appearances conform to his needs as a capitalist.

The structure providentially provides itself with all that it needs to be set in motion.

But having sent his capitalist to the school of the apparent motion, Rancière soon recognises that there is no learning by a pure perception:

> The capitalist *has no reason* to concern himself with the internal structure of the process. The categories which he *needs* are those which express the forms of the apparent notion in which he lives and *carries out his calculations*. The constitutive category of the process are for him the rubrics of his account book.
>
> *TP* 6 (p. 39) (my emphasis)

We see here the same functionalist and rationalist conception of the subject—whose reasons and needs are given him by the structure and which represent certain necessary functions of the structure. But we also find this rational subject carrying out calculations and possessing account books. Calculations, account books, etc., are not the mere material auxiliaries of a perception; they designate the presence of a practice which cannot be reduced to *experience* and *intuition*. Calculation is no more a mere faculty of the subject, account books no more a mere convenience to record what the subject perceives, than Galileo's telescope was a mere medium between his eye and the truth in the stars.

Rancière registers the *fact* that capitalists undertake calculation and use accounting techniques but he makes nothing of it. These *facts* overturn his whole conception of the capitalist subject and his perceptions. The forms of calculation are not spontaneously given to the capitalist as the faculties of a rational subject by his intuition and experience of the process. These forms are not guaranteed in the subjectivity of a place. While a practice of calculation is structurally necessary to the process production-circulation-reproduction its forms are not directly provided by that process. The existence of such forms is a condition of existence of capitalism, but they are not given in the structure simply because they are necessary to the structure. Calculation as a practice depends upon 'knowledge' and bodies of technique which have a history, which vary in their form, and have different specific circumstances of origin. The conditions of their existence (for example, the development of double-entry book keeping) are not given in the structure of the capitalist mode of production in general. Accountancy is a specific discipline which any capitalist must master and in which he must be *trained* (unless he employs a trained functionary) – he does not intuit its necessity and its operations from his experience as a capitalist. If he were to do so he would be a capitalist *before* he became a calculator – he would enter his place as a *tabula rasa*. Rancière does in fact explicitly state that the knowledges necessary to the capitalist follow from his place:

> The place of the agents of production in the process thus determines the necessary representations of their practice as *mere expressions* of the apparent motion of capital.
>
> *TP* 6 (p. 41) (my emphasis)

For Rancière there is one given capitalist rationality-ideology and but one possible effectivity of that subjectivity of the place. Capitalist ideology is an invariant given of the structure of capitalism, eternal, unchanging and always identical in its effects. It always makes these experiential imprints on those blank subjects. But it is possible to argue that, while certain things must be calculated and represented by the capitalist, the mode in which this is done can differ considerably and the mode can have effects which are far from equivalent. There is, for example, no logical reason why a capitalist or capitalists should not attempt to found their practice on the knowledges of *Capital*. To take Rancière's example of the relations of wages and prices, according to him the capitalist must *see* wages as a cost. Wages are indeed a cost to the capitalist in that he must pay a wages bill. There is absolutely no reason why, however, while registering wage costs in his accounting procedures, the capitalist may not (having read *Capital*) suppose that the labour power he sets to work creates surplus value for him. The capitalist can then try to seek measures which both reduce his wages bill to the minimum and maximise the production of surplus value. Various other ideologies and bases of calculation are possible – social moralist ideologies of a just wage, a just price, moral limits to profitability etc. – these may affect individual capitalist's practices and calculations for good or ill (Robert Owen prospered from the putting into economic practice of such social moralist ideologies). Why capitalists do not read *Capital*, why a predominant ideological articulation exists, are problems which cannot be solved by an appeal to the necessities of the structure. This appeal is necessarily teleological and rests on a rationalist humanism. The predominance of certain ideologies must be explained by a complex account respecting the determinations at the various levels (economic, political, ideological, etc.) and recognising that the capitalist mode of production has arisen in and been generalised from certain specific social formations. It is a confusion of levels of analysis to conflate the necessity of ideological articulation in the structure of the mode of production in general with the specific ideologies which are articulated in the case of a particular social formation in which that mode exists.

Rancière does not respect this latter condition. He denies in effect any necessity of an articulation between the economic and the ideological instances in capitalism. For him the structure of the capitalist process automatically generates its own motors and motives, its own illusions and ideological conditions of existence. Rancière's position amounts to the autonomisation of the economy in the production of 'its' ideology, the autonomy and self-action of the economy as a complete system, and the practical abolition of the ideological instance. Taken to its logical extreme and presented as a theory of ideology Rancière's position is *economistic*.

3 Fetishism

In his discussion of the fetishism on which the Trinity Formula rests Rancière argues that interest-bearing capital is an *a-conceptual* form; a form characterised by the disappearance of the process in its result. In *Capital* the movement of *objectification* has the following structure: the a-conceptual form which is the result of the process is autonomised, it becomes a given thing in itself, this objectification-autonomisation provides the foundation for the *subjectivisation* of the thing in which the form into which the real process has vanished then presents itself as an autonomous subject which determines its own behaviour and which is its own cause. This a-conceptual form is, Rancière claims, the most radical effect of metonymic causality; the couple relation/form, *Darstellung/Vorstellung* characterising this causality. Rancière argues that the objectification-subjectification structure in *Capital* is different in essence from formally similar structures in the *1844 Manuscripts*.

Rancière does not pose the problem that a non-anthropological Hegelian logic may be present in *Capital* – that Hegelianism is not a mere matter of humanism and the presence of a constitutive subject. Rancière argues that in *Capital* the subject-predicates-object structure of the *1844 Manuscripts* does not exist because: in *Capital* a substantial subject is not the support of the movement's objectification-subjectification, and the discourse of *Capital* is not closed by pre-given anthropological premises as is that of *1844*. There is no alienation in *Capital*, no alienation of a substantial subject, Rancière has indeed proved that, but if the relations lose nothing to the form, if they do not lose themselves in it, it is because they remain *behind* the form. The relations cannot play the part of the alienated subject, for they never cease to be what they are. The relations are the *secret* of the form, and the form is the phenomenal form the relations take. The logic of this analysis of the commodity, an analysis which depends upon theoretical devices of an analogous structure to that of *1843/1844* – hypostatisation, objectification-subjectification, real and apparent motion, etc, – tends toward that of essence and appearance. Despite the different theoretical *functions* these homologous and analogous theoretical structures have to play in *Capital* they retain the *places* of their Hegelian and Young Marxist youth – used as forms to think the action of a structural causality they have obvious inadequacies. Using these forms a real distance is created by the action of this 'metonymic' causality, in which the relation is not inscribed in the form, in which the form becomes a mere device of concealment of the relation, and in which this distance makes the one phenomenal and apparent, the other determinant and real. The absence of the cause from its effects is clear here; its mode of presence in them is more uncertain.

Rancière does pose the problem of the presence of Hegelian forms in *Capital* in the form of a particular problem – Marx's confusion of the *Entfremdung* of the relation in the form with the alienation of the subject's predicates in the *1844 Manuscripts*. Rancière does not raise as a problem the conditions of existence of this slide from one discourse into another, the presence of the forms of one discourse in another. For Rancière such slides are a function of the failure of the localisation-definition of concepts. The words which express the concepts are common to the *1844 Manuscripts* and *Capital*:

> That is, anthropology has no place in *Capital* except the one kept for it by relapses in Marx's discourse. Where Marx fails to locate his concepts the latter arrange themselves around anthropological reference points. Where the rigour of his discourse slackens we see an anthropological model emerge. Such slides necessarily occur insofar as Marx does not rigorously criticize his vocabulary. The words which express the new concepts introduced by *Capital* are in many cases the same as those which expressed the anthropoligical concepts of the young Marx.
>
> *Economy and Society*, vol. 5 No. 3 (p. 364)

Therefore the presence of a *word* is sufficient to generate the confusion of *concepts* which Rancière argues are different. The slide from one concept to the other is a function of the absence of a rigorous terminology:

> Rigour therefore requires that the words in which these relational concepts are expressed should likewise be different.

As Marx does not meet this demand for rigour, the first form (*figure*) always threatens to insinuate itself where it no longer has any place.

E & S (p. 364)

Rancière almost seems to rely on an associationist psychology at this point: the 'author' of the discourse slips into another train of thought, a slip triggered by the presence of a familiar word. Later on Rancière argues that the absence of a rigorous terminology is 'not simply negligence', that it stems from a non-demarcation of *Capital* and the *1844 Manuscripts*, a failure to reflect in adequate *terms* the break separating the discourse of *Capital* from that of the Young Marx. This locates the problem simply in Marx's failure to auto-reflect his discourse in a philosophy. Thus in differentiating between the two *Entfremdungs*, the two theoretical spaces of *Capital* and the Young Marx, Rancière fails to recognise the presence, within *Capital* itself, of Hegelian conceptual forms. Rancière's text in fact contributes to their misconception in so far as he establishes them on a firm anti-humanist basis, and differentiates them from the works of 1843–44.

Thus we encounter, in these examples taken from Rancière's text in which questions of ideology are raised, the following positions: (i) ideology as a structure-effect; (ii) the theory of ideology as a perception of a misleading object by a subject, and the concept of *experience* which links the concrete subject with the place of perception; (iii) the tendency for an essence-appearance model to replace structural causality, and for the effects of the structure to be reduced to the status of a *screen*.

C MILLER – 'THE FUNCTION OF THEORETICAL TRAINING'

An analogous theory of ideology to that of Rancière is to be found in Jacques-Alain Miller's short text 'The Function of Theoretical Training':

In the structural system in which production is articulated in a
specific mode, the zone of displacement of the subject – in so far
as the structure concedes it the perception of its state (of its
apparent motion) while stealing that of the system – is defined
as *illusion*. The latter, in so far as the subject reflects it, signifies
it, in a word reduplicates it, perpetuates itself in the form of
ideology. Illusion and ideology, if they are thought in the
continuity of a 'seeing' to a 'telling' form the element natural to
a subject rigorously qualified by its insertion into the structure
of a social formation. Precisely because the economy is *the last
instance*, to be situated as the referent of all the manifestations of
social practice, its action is radically foreign to the dimension
of the current (*actuel*), it offers itself by its effects. The absence
of the cause is enough to achieve the inversion of the structural
determination at the level of the individual consciousness. As
perception the inversion is illusion. As discourse ideology.

TP 6 (p. 49)

Miller ascribes the *illusion* of the subject's perception to its
presence in a 'state' of the structure, the concrete existence of the
structure. Ideology is a secondary elaboration of this illusory
perception – its transformation into discourse. The structure
duplicates the gap between the conditions of production of the
effects and the conditions of their perception which we en-
countered in Rancière's text. In Miller the level of the ideological
effect is different: here it is the action of the 'metonymic causality'
of the structuration of a mode of production. Despite the change
of level this conception of ideology is the same as and as
problematical as that concerning the commodity-form. The
principal defect of this conception is that it secretes a subject into
the structure, a subject whose *means* of perception are not to be
found in the structural place the subject occupies (only the object
which generates misrecognition by being perceived is given in
that place) but in the human subject which is smuggled into that
place. The subject which *sees* the phenomena of the structure is
endowed with the obviousness of a *sight*, an obviousness we
hardly notice. For Miller individual subjects are given as

spectators to the ruses of the structure, just as the spectators of the apparent motions of the planets are 'given' on the surface of the earth. The subject is like the empiricist conception of the star-gazer, the eye faced with given objects, and like his cousin he exists outside of ideology and the ideological instance as a perceiving subject. There is nothing ideological about the subject's sight, it is merely the place he occupies which is misleading. The subject is prior to ideology.

Althusser's interiorisation of the subject within the ideological instance necessarily changes the terms of the theory of ideology: the source of ideology is no longer sought in the perception by a subject of objects given in the world, but in the relation of the instances one to another and in the internal structure of the ideological instance. Instead of the relation structure → subject it is the relation of the ideological instance to the global structuration of the instances and the necessities of ideological articulation generated by the regional structurations of the other instances. In Miller's text the existence of ideology as an instance or as a practice is problematical: ideology is forever given by the way a structure is structured, it is not an instance but a concomitant shadow of the structure. In Miller's text the effectivity of this structure effect depends in turn upon humanist suppositions – upon a subject pre-given to the structure with the natural faculties of man.

5 The Law of Property and Marxism

The Marxist theory of law conceives it as a 'superstructure' brought into existence by the private possession of the means of production and the consequent division of society into classes. Law as analysed in Marxist theory is divided into the two distinct social functions which it performs: the function of regulation of relations of possession and the function of regulation of the struggle between the classes. The regulation of possession gives to existing relations of production the form of right: it is their 'legal expression' and gives a definite form to relations between possessors and to relations between them and non-possessors. The legal regulation of the class struggle serves to contain and repress the antagonism of the exploited class within the forms of right legitimated by the order of the state. Marxism conceives this division as a difference of *functions*, a difference which takes specific institutional forms in the different modes of production. Thus in the feudal mode there is no equivalent of the capitalist distinction of public and private law: relations of possession between members of the dominant class are defined and regulated as right to *political* domain and office, and relations with the subordinate classes fuse exploiter and state functionary in the person of the seigneur who presides at the manorial court.

The Marxist theory of law tends to divide law as subject to two different sets of exigencies and explained by two relatively distinct bodies of theory. The first set of exigencies concerns the regulation of possession: law in giving *expression* to already existing production relations provides certain conditions of their operation, it gives these relations a definite form as right, regulates disputes over possession and assigns (in defining property) a definite place and obligations to the propertyless (slave, serf, seller of labour power, etc.). The theory which explains these exigencies is the theory of the mode of production and of the conditions of its operation. The *form* of right here is functionally important to the economy: it must correspond to and express the dominant relations of production. The second set of exigencies concern the maintenance of class rule: law is the form in which individual and collective acts of resistance by the subordinate classes are repressed. The theory deployed here is that of the state as 'representative' and guarantor of class society. The *form* of right here is wholly encompassed by its *ideological* function. Legality is necessary to the normal functioning of the state in its 'constitutional' form (feudal, liberal, or whatever), but in conditions of acute class struggle this legality is dispensed with and replaced by brute and unlimited force. The Marxist theory of the state attempts to reveal this continuing action of class force behind the screen of legal-constitutional ideology. In analysing property right Marxist theory attempts to demonstrate its *ideological* function, it legitimises existing production relations, but also its *economic* function, it is not pure ideology but an ideological condition of operation of the economy (the *forms* it involves cannot be dispensed with as pure illusions, they must be replaced by others). Law is uncovered as an economic necessity and as a cloak for class violence.[1] Both forms of analysis reduce the legal forms to exigencies of the mode of production of which they are an effect. However, the mode of attribution of effect and the way law is regarded tend to differ.

This discussion will be concerned with the Marxist theory of the law of property and its limitations. The preceding remarks serve to indicate that it has tended to be a specific field within Marxist theory, separate from the theory of the state and the mode of analysis of law subsumed therein. This separation has a number of important consequences. Firstly, although legal codes and institutions require legislative action within a form of state, the classic Marxist theories of property law pay little attention to the place of origin of law within the state. The genesis of law is explained in terms of the functional exigencies of the mode of production: law is their 'expression' and the mode of legislation is at best a secondary matter.

Secondly, Marxist theoretical analyses of the function of regulating possession have concentrated on commodity/ capitalist forms of property law. The institutional separation of public and private law, and of criminal and civil law creates the autonomy of *legal* spheres which makes plausible the separation of analysis into two bodies of theory concerned with different functions of law and legality.

Thirdly, in the analysis of capitalist property law, institutional autonomy of civil law permits Marxism's identification of the economic subject and the subject of right – treating the latter as merely a necessary expression – form of the former.

The Marxist theory of the law of property has concentrated on commodity/capitalist legal relations, in which the function of the regulation of possession is differentiated within the body of the law into a distinct institutional realm. It explains the conditions of existence of the *content* of this realm and of its differentiation with the body of the law by reference to the needs and circumstances of an economy of independent private producers brought into relation with one another through individual acts of exchange of their products.

This conception of an economy of independent private producers, economic subjects, possessors of the products of socially divided labours, brought into relation through exchange, serves to explain a realm of independent legal subjects, the possessors of rights, who confront one another in the sphere of legal regulation. But this conception entails a particular notion of the economic subject, and, therefore, a particular concept of the limits of possession with the forms of commodity/capitalist property law. This notion of economic subject and the conception of economy from which it derives sets a limit on the forms of property right possible within capitalism. It limits the analysis of property law and capitalist organisation: assigning to both an essence of the relations of production which it is their function to express.

This abstract point can be illustrated by a specific example, the joint-stock company and other corporate forms of ownership of capital. By means of this example I will demonstrate the general theoretical conditions of the Marxist explanation of the law of property which lead it to a halt before this limit. The Marxist theory of the law of property gives a privileged place to a certain form of organisation of units of production or enterprises in capitalism: the subject of property right, the subject actually possessing the means of production, and the subject who engages in economic calculation and exchange all coincide in the person of the 'capitalist'. The capitalist is the archetypical and necessary form of capitalist economic organisation; the displacement of this coincidence of subjects in an individual human subject signals that the limits of capitalist relations of production have been reached. Marxist economic and legal theory has been unable to come to terms with the joint-stock company or corporation *as a form of economic organisation in capitalism*. Further, it cannot come to terms with the fact that this form of organisation has specific legal conditions of existence. This inability is in no way overcome by the concept of 'monopoly capital', for this is merely one of the forms of *failure* to deal with corporate capitalism.[2] To the extent that it does consider the corporate form it regards it as *necessarily transitional*, as a sign of the negation of capitalist relations of production. The units of production organised under this form of capital (a form regarded by most Marxists as a functionless survival of private property) are conceived as distinct from this form, as anticipations of socialised production. This analysis disvalues the corporation as an organisational form *of* capitalism and cannot come to terms with its economic-organisational effects: the units of production made possible by this organisational form are *capitalist* in their structure, technique and operations and they cannot be regarded as anticipations of socialist forms of enterprise.

It will be argued that this failure is not confined to subsequent interpreters who have built up the Marxist theory of the law of property, rather it stems from the basic theory of the economic subject in *Capital*. It is Marx's concept of the capitalist mode of production which gives a particular form of economic organisation and a particular conception of property right its privileged place. The classic Marxist theories of the law of property have built directly on the theory of the economic subject in *Capital*, regarding the legal form as an 'expression' of this subject. The problem is not one of deviation from but one of loyalty to Marx.

Here texts by two leading exponents of the Marxist theory of the law of property, E. B. Pashukanis (*The General Theory of Law and Marxism*) and Karl Renner (*The Institutions of Private Law and Their Social Functions*) will be considered. The position on property right I am criticising is no aberration of one particular and divergent 'school' of Marxists. Pashukanis and Renner represent very different theoretical and political positions within Marxism. Renner, a leading Austro-Marxist, adopts a neo-Kantian positivist conception of scientific method and accepts the theory of legal formalism (whose main representative was Hans Kelsen) which argues that the law is an autonomous sphere of concepts and that legal institutions must be analysed as constructions of pure legality without reference to their use in legal practice. Pashukanis uses Marx's '1857 Introduction' to *A Contribution to the Critique of Political Economy* in a brilliant and skilful way to present an independent methodological basis in legal theory. He rejects formalism and yet seeks a way to explain the specific nature of the legal realm. He seeks a Marxist explanation of law which accounts for and does not merely reduce its existence as a distinct sphere. In his conception of capitalist economy Pashukanis shares many similarities with his contemporary and compatriot I. I. Rubin (*Essays on Marx's Theory of Value*).[3]

The similarity in Renner's and Pashukanis' conception of the determination of property right stems not from methodology or legal philosophy but from a common relation to *Capital*. Renner and Pashukanis, like their economist countrymen Hilferding and Rubin, concentrate on the conception in *Capital* of a society in which socially divided and independent labours are united in exchange. Society as an organised structure of divided labour realises itself only through the unplanned intersubjectivity of exchange, property law is one of the 'fetish' forms of expression of this process which at the same time makes it possible.

This conception of property right as an 'expression' of social relations borne by an individual subject and necessary to his (socially determined) practice in those relations is not a mere relic of the twenties and thirties. It is still current. It is in substance the position taken by an Althusserian theorist like Bernard Edelman (*La Droit saisi par la photographie*).[4]

Before proceeding it is necessary to indicate what is at stake in this criticism. We are not concerned merely with a limited and 'abstract' region of Marxist theory. I am criticising this Marxist conception of property right (and capitalist organisation as reflected in it) because of the limits it imposes on the analysis of modern capitalism. The corporation, far from being a transitional phenomenon, is the dominant form of organisation of capitalist production. This *organisational form* has important effects on the way capitalist production is carried on. It cannot be dismissed as an administrative or legal detail. Property law in capitalism is not (and has not been) confined to the conditions of the triple coincidence of property, possession and calculation outlined above. Corporate organisation and property law, legal institutions and economic organisation are not one and the same thing. However, the existing state of Marxist theory of the economic and the legal subject sets obstacles to the analysis of capitalist organisation and property law; it cannot come to terms with forms whose process of development has only just begun. Theoretical changes are necessary if we are to follow this development in theory and come to terms with it in political practice.

This chapter is organised into four sections:

(1) The Theory of Economic Subjectivity in *Capital*;
(2) Property and Commodity Fetishism: A. Pashukanis and B. Renner;
(3) Marx on the Joint Stock Company;
(4) Why the Legal Form of Corporate Property is Politically Important.

1 THE THEORY OF ECONOMIC SUBJECTIVITY IN CAPITAL

In order to comprehend Marx's concept of the capitalist as economic subject it is necessary to recognise the system of social relations in which it is operative. My co-authors and I have discussed Marx's concept of social totality in some detail in *Marx's Capital and Capitalism Today* and so I will be brief, and I hope not too cryptic, here. Capital constructs a concept of a social totality, the capitalist mode of production. This totality is conceived, following the methodology of the '1857 Introduction', as an 'appropriation of the concrete in thought': a concept which expresses in abstraction the effectivity of the real itself. This conception of totality as reality appropriated in abstraction entails a reality appropriate to abstraction. In order for a totality and its effects to be expressible in abstraction the totality must include the causes of these effects within itself: it must be *its own determination*, at one with its effects. It becomes a finite unity of being, an entity which subsumes all the effects of its domain. Such an entity cannot admit of conditions of its own existence and effects pertinent to it which are not given in its concept. To do so would be to make it dependent upon a reality outside of its abstraction and reduce to incoherence the knowledge process in which it is postulated. Such a totality-concept has two attributes which concern us here:

(i) It establishes a set of *limits*. The totality is a reality made finite by the necessary internality of its own causation. The totality cannot exceed certain limits of structural form and effect and remain itself: if it produces effects beyond its structure then these are contradictions and signal the conditions of existence of a new and distinct totality within the old. The totality-entity is limited in the development of its social relations to those given as necessary to it in its concept.

(ii) It follows that to exist as its concept (in the form of abstraction) the totality must *secure its own conditions of existence* and subordinate its effects. It must determine itself and its own action by producing all the effects which are necessary to its own functioning. It reduces the effects in its domain to effects of or effects appropriate to itself.

How does the capitalist mode of production (CMP), a totality of this class, secure its own conditions of existence? The answer is to be found in the classic concepts of historical materialism, outlined in the '1859 Preface': that the economy determines the form taken by social relations and that these social relations are made by men but in a manner independent of their will. The CMP is a totality composed of *social relations between men*. Its action as a totality consists in imposing a definite manner of acting upon men which is independent of their will. Because the CMP consists of relations between human subjects it follows that to secure its conditions of existence is to impose definite structurally conditioned forms at the level of subjectivity and inter-subjectivity. Given the premise of historical materialism ('The mode of production of material life conditions the social, political and intellectual life process in general'), the construction of an adequate concept of economy, explaining the modes of its action on other social relations, is the construction of a concept of totality.

The mode in which the capitalist economy secures the non-economic conditions of its existence (and thereby becomes an effective totality) is explained by the theory of 'fetishism'. 'Fetishism' is the form in which subjects 'enter into relations which are independent of their will' and which as *inter-subjectivity* serve to reproduce the structure of the whole.

These 'relations' constitute a series of *places* (capitalist, worker, etc.).[5] The totality is represented by a series of 'personifications' of social functions, character masks which stand for the various economic agents and classes. Individual human subjects are allocated to those places and interiorise through the experience of the place the character mask appropriate to it. The place involves a 'point of view' of social relations which secretes a way of thinking and acting appropriate to its location in the structure. Thus the 'capitalist', the bearer of capital, is conceived as representing a mere fragment or moment of the totality of capital; a fragment set in motion by the experiences it has in common with other fragments. The capitalist is a 'mere aliquot part' of the total social capital, a part which calculates and acts, and the movement of the whole is effected through and as the experiences and actions it impresses on its bearers.

Capitalism, like all commodity production, is a division of labour between independent producers who are linked by the exchanges of their products one with another. Production is unplanned and socially atomised and is socialised through the process of the exchange of products and its effects. Men appear socially (inter-subjectively) as the bearers of their products-commodities – and relate to one another through the exchange of those products. Capitalist and worker in like fashion appear as buyers and sellers of commodities. The commodity/capitalist economy is the first social form in which 'economic' relations are differentiated as a distinct and autonomous sphere of life. This autonomy corresponds to the independence of men as producers and possessors of commodities and to the specific form of their interdependence in the exchange of things. Social relations between men appear as exchanges between things.

Through this system of *places* and exchanges between the possessors of things the capitalist mode of production generates all the conditions necessary to the reproduction of its division of the labour of society and its social process of exploitation. Men as character masks corresponding to places and as bearers of commodities create the subjective and inter-subjective conditions of existence of capitalist society in the forms appropriate to its limits.

Two consequences follow from this mode in which the non-economic conditions of its operation are generated by the action of the economic structure itself. Firstly, central to the generation of the subjective conditions of capitalist relations, the 'personification' of the places in its structure, is the concept of 'experience'. Individual human subjects occupy places and interiorise, through *experience*, the appearances given to this point of perception of the process (appearances which serve as the basis of actions of the subject which are necessary to the structure). It follows that the economic subjects by means of which the system is put in motion must be entities capable of 'experience' that is, individual human subjects. (Or rather, we should note here, a particular *concept* of individual humans as subjects – the empty subject who interiorises his essence through experience. *Capital* requires a conception of economic subject which entails the attributes of Locke's concept of the knowing subject – doubtless we shall be told Locke's concept reflects the mutilated but necessary form of man in commodity fetishism.) *Capital's* conception of the way the economy secures its non-economic conditions of existence makes it virtually impossible to conceive of economic subjects which are not directly represented by human subjects. Corporate agencies are almost without exception regarded within Marxism as being reducible to the actions of functionaries who take the place of the personification 'capitalist'.

For the structure of capitalist economy in *Capital* to operate, relations between economic enterprises must be reducible to relations between human subjects mediated through their experience.

Secondly, from this it follows that definite limits are set on the form and conditions of capitalist economic calculation. Calculation is an effect of experience, it is the interiorisation of the appearances generated by the structure and action on the basis of these appearances. Calculation is an effect of the structure, an effect which continues the structure's existence through the generation of appropriate subjective behaviours and the results of those behaviours. For calculation to work in this way and to perform this social function supposes a *universal subject* of calculation and a *given content of calculation*. A universal subject of calculation: for all subjects placed in the same position to experience and to act in modes appropriate to the structure they must have the same constitution, the same modes of perception and the same processes of reasoning to act on them. Necessary and given economic effects require identical and homogenous subjects who support those effects. Marxism is not different from neo-classical economic theory in constructing a representative economic actor (it is the attributes and actions of this actor which differ). A given content of calculation: the course of action to be followed is given in the appearance-form which is generated by the structure, the structure therefore creates within itself the calculative categories necessary to its existence. Once the attributes of the subjects who calculate, the mode of their calculation and the conditions in which they calculate are differentiated and are not given by the structure of the economy then the calculative results and their effects can differ. *Capital* cannot admit of this difference for it would shatter the conditions necessary to conceive the existence of capitalism as concrete generality. In *Capital* actions and calculations at enterprise level are indifferent, they are submerged in the movements and determinants of the total social capital, the mere fragments of which they are. *Capital* discounts the differential effectivity of enterprises and its conditions as a possible or investigable problem. It is necessary to recognise that enterprises do differ in organisational form, in calculative method and content, and in the conditions of calculation. A substantial portion of Marx's *Capital and Capitalism Today*, Vol. 2, is devoted to demonstrating this – space prevents its repetition here. However, the specific effects of different types of capitalist organisation raise important economic and political issues to which we will return briefly in our discussion of why company law matters to socialists, at the end of this paper.

2   PROPERTY AND COMMODITY FETISHISM

A   *Pashukanis*

Pashukanis sets out in *The General Theory of Law and Marxism* to explain law in the specificity of its form. Bourgeois legal theories (natural law, formalism, etc.) recognise the specificity of the form but either eternalise it as a representation of fundamental values, or convert it into an abstract ideality, a product of juridic reason.

What is required is a *materialist* explanation of the specific form. Here, however, Pashukanis breaks with the vulgar materialism which was becoming dominant in the USSR in his day. Pashukanis appeals to Marx's '1857 Introduction' as the support for his method – his reading of this text is most perceptive and he makes brilliant use of it. Science proceeds by the formation of determinate abstractions, and by the successive development of these abstract forms appropriates the concrete. Scientific analysis does not follow the order of its historical development to comprehend a social form, rather it analyses through the most developed form its essence and, therefore, the conditions of its genealogy. Pashukanis insists on the specificity of the legal *form* and, thereby, breaks with a dominant tendency in 'materialist' analysis, the reduction of law to the state and to class coercion. In this reduction the specific social necessity of the *form* of law disappears, it becomes mere legality, a legitimisation for class oppression. Pashukanis counters his colleague the Soviet jurist Stuchka who took up this position as follows:

> Law no longer figures in this general formula furnished by Stuchka as a *specific* social relationship; its character . . . *is that of a system of relationships which answers the interests of the dominant class and of safeguarding that class with organised force* . . . It discloses the class content comprised in juridic forms, but fails to explain why this content takes such a form.
>
> Pashukanis (p. 140 – emphasis in original)

The echo of Marx's strictures on Ricardo's analysis of value will not be missed by the reader; Pashukanis draws deeply from the methodology and analyses of *Capital* to provide the foundations of his conception of materialist explanation. Law, like value, is a *form*. In order to comprehend a form (be it law or value or whatever) it is necessary to begin by constructing the concept of its simplest and most general nature and proceed from this general concept to the more complex forms of its concrete existence. This general concept for Pashukanis is contained in the fact that the subject of law is the bearer of a right.

It is this general concept that enables Pashukanis to claim to have differentiated (analytically and not merely conventionally – in terms of institutions) public and private law and to insist that private law defines the essence of the legal form. Right in private law can only be understood by analogy with possession – right is an attribute (a defining characteristic) of the legal subject. It is in pursuit or defence of a right that its possessor appears in law and it is as the sphere of regulation of this possession between subjects that the law itself comes into existence.

Public law is a *juridicisation* of the state, it is a conception of the state in the forms of law. The concept of 'right of parliament' is confused and contradictory, either it equates right and power, the capacity to command, or it operates by analogy with private right (pp. 155–6). The organs of the state cannot be conceived, however, as possessive subjects of right or as the origin of the concept of subject. Pashukanis remarks:

> State law can exist solely as a reflection of the private law form in the sphere of political organisation or it ceases in general to be law. Any attempt to depict a social function as that which it is . . . and a norm as simply an organised rule, means the death of the legal form. (p. 156)

He thus rejects the concept of law as imperative or command (which he argues in its bourgeois form makes the conception of state or society issuing the command a transcendental one or a subject-person, and in its Marxist form reduces law to mere ideology, a cloak for class rule) in favour of the concept of law as possessive right.[6] Pashukanis conceives private law as having an origin independent of state legislative action, as arising from necessities independent of the sphere of the political as such. Here is an attempt to defend by serious theoretical arguments as to the nature and form of law the unimportance of its apparent place of origin in state legislation. Private law is an organic social form not the creation of a legislative act. The state itself takes its legislative and constitutional 'juridic' form from analogies with the sphere of private law and private right.

Thus we see Pashukanis intelligently and vigorously defending the separation in Marxist analysis between the conception of law as property right and as class coercion. This defence rests on two theoretical conditions.

Firstly, to define law as possessive right and not as imperative rule rests on a particular conception of the social origin of the form. The separation of private law and the state, the subordination of the apparent place of origin of law in legislative action, is possible only on the basis of a particular concept of social totality. That concept is of an economy-totality which secures its own conditions of existence through its action on its subjects. The forms from which law derives are represented by the social process to the agents. The economic as objective process secretes the categories and contents necessary to consciousness (reality engenders its own representations – it signifies itself in definite forms).[7] Fetishism is this process of auto-signification by the real, a signification interiorised by the subject-supports of social relations. It is this auto-signification as an effect of the whole which permits the dismissal of the pertinence of the apparent origin of law in legislation. The criticism converts legislation into an *origin*, asking where law 'comes from' makes it permissible to ridicule legislation as a constitutive act of creation. Some legal philosophers do entertain this fancy. But what makes this conception of legislation-as-origin possible is the particular properties of the Marxist concept of totality in *Capital*. This concept is of a unity of being governed by the principle of the interiority of its effects. In this conception law must have an *origin* (a single determinative principle) in order for it to correspond to a place and function within the whole. Law without an origin, not ascribed to the action of some element of the totality and irreducible to its principle, would threaten the action of its causality and the knowledge process which that causality corresponds to. Inconsistent with the totality, outside its effects, it threatens its existence as concrete generality appropriable in abstraction. It is no accident that Pashukanis draws on the methodology of the '1857 Introduction' and *Capital*, his concept of law depends on them.

Once this concept of a totality as a unity interiorising its effects (and therefore being constrained by consistency-limits) is rejected, the problem of legislation is not so easily solved by giving it the stigma of origin. Pashukanis' posing of the *form* of law as a problem can be turned against him. He uses this concept of law as form to establish the specificity of legal norms and to avoid their reduction to command and class oppression. But his construction and defence of the form also involves a particular content: in being defined in its form law is given a unitary origin, nature and social function. Possessive right, the essence of the legal form, is a derivative of commodity relations between economic subjects. One reductionism, of law to class oppression, is rejected in the interests of another, of legal form to commodity form. Following Pashukanis' own strategy may we not ask of him why law must be given an organic origin in civil society which reduces the process of legislation to the status of a mere phenomenal form or phantom? Is not the origin of and operation of the laws within a specific set of apparatuses itself a specific form which requires explanation?

The challenge to the concept of social totality employed by Pashukanis also challenges the legitimacy of his particular reductive account of law. If it is accepted that the legal, calculative and other conditions of existence of a mode or relations of production are not provided by any necessary process of representation to the agents which is internal to their structure then this raises the question of how these conditions are defined, determined and met. The removal of this concept of totality (as a self-determining entity) removes the need and the theoretical foundation for a single origin to and form of those conditions. Legislation, to be pertinent to the definition and analysis of law, need no longer be conceived as an *origin* – as the point of creation of a unified set of categories with a single social function. Law is no longer assigned a single and pre-given social content which it must express. The conditions under which, say, capitalist relations of production operate are no longer determined by the necessary action of those relations themselves. Thus the laws regulating property ownership, wages, hours of work, etc., will effect in some measure the way those relations are defined and operate. These laws are not in principle derivable from the operation or necessities of those relations themselves.

Pashukanis' concept of law mirrors that of the idealist legal philosophies he opposes. In defining law as form he seeks a common defining essence of the legal sphere. Likewise, conceptions of law as the representative of ethical values or as a system inspired by juridic rationality give the law an essence, a common content and object which expresses a unitary necessity or cause outside it (values, reason, etc.). Pashukanis counters transcendental and subjectivist concepts of the origin of law with a 'materialist' concept of organic social origin. Yet he attempts to give legal norms a single general form and content. Hence he employs the classical legal-philosophical opposition of legal norms to commands. Seeking to assign law an essence-in-origin necessarily gives it a single content. Forms called 'laws' which diverge from this content-essence are considered as secondary elaborations, or perversions. Seeking to assign an essence-content to law creates a category of law-in-general (what law *is*); this can be different and divergent from particular laws and legal institutions. Law-in-general can thus disvalue legislation (laws contradict the essence of law). This potentiality of divergence between the concept of law and legislation has served legal philosophers as a basis for ethical and political critique (for example, such uses of the doctrines of natural law and natural rights). Pashukanis, of course, is not seeking to use the category of law-in-general in this way, but it has similar effects, the privileging of the general category and the disvaluing of legislation.

If, on the contrary, we begin the analysis of law by *not* seeking to assign it a single essence-content then we are forced to take the legislative process and legal institutions seriously. The laws have no necessary unity of content, form or function *outside* of that derived from the legislative process and legal apparatuses. *Laws can be divergent and inconsistent in form and function and remain laws*. The question switches to that of the nature and effectivity of legislative/legal systems. This means considering the process of enactment and adjudication of the conditions necessary to them, and the effects they produce. The general categories for such an analysis must be limited to specifying what is involved in the determination of those processes and conditions. What law and legality is cannot be defined as a general concept independent of legal system. Laws, legislation and the categories involved in these institutions define what law is. Legal institutions work through and as definite bodies of discourse (although they and their effects are not reducible to discourse and discursive effects); definite categories are part of the action of these institutions as social relations. Law is defined in and by its discourses and categories.

Legislation and legal apparatuses become the points of departure in the analysis of law. It is by being enacted, codified, subjected to dispute and interpretation that laws and the nature of legality are defined and developed. Law is a social practice taking place within particular apparatuses and by means of a particular type of discourse. Practice, apparatuses and discourse can develop within legal systems and differ between them. The concept of law-in-general essentialises the laws and prevents the analysis of law as a social practice. It ascribes the essence to conditions outside it and which are determinative of it as essence (relations of production, ethics, reason etc.). The constraints of a given general content compel the reduction of the law to necessities outside it (only in this way can its determination be made compatible with its essence). Assigning a definitive effectivity to legislation and legal practice means that law can outrun and redefine its discursive and categoric forms.

Legislation is pertinent as a point of departure and legal discourse is pertinent as a definition of existing forms of the law. But a point of departure is not the point of termination. Legislation is not an origin. Legislation and legal apparatuses are effective on the law as a process with a definite institutional and discursive form. As a form due legislative procedure is necessary to law, it cannot have the effect of legality without it. Similarly, judgements and interpretations proceed under definite forms and conditions of discourse. The essentialist thesis is correct in one respect, laws do differ from other rules. They do not differ in essence but in the form and effects of the institutions issuing and practising them. Analysis of the specificity of legal rules is the analysis of the constitution of definite spheres of activity confined within and conditional on certain apparatuses. The nature of legislative procedure, the conditions of access to it, etc., effect the content of the law. To conceive the law as certain institutions and practices is to raise the question of their conditions of existence and operation.

Legislation, far from being an origin, is something which requires *explanation*, but not *reduction*. Law and legislation must be conceived as processes. Marx defines a process in *Capital* as the 'synthesis of many determinations'. Law can best be conceived in this way. Legislation and law are procedures and forms upon which many determinations act (to produce particular enactments, judgements, etc.) – legal apparatuses and discourses impose constraints of procedure, form and discourse on these determinations. The process of legislation has attached to it conditions of access and operation, and through these conditions many and varying influences and circumstances express themselves. The conditions and influences acting upon the process are effective and are given form through its procedures. Conditions and influences are not themselves legal forms or effects: it is only through and as legislation and legal practice that they are effective. Legislation is not an expression, it is translation into another and specific language. Legislation and law as specific practices impose constraints and limits on the political, economic, moral, etc., objectives sought through them. The degree and form of these constraints, and of the conditions of access to legislation and adjudication, vary considerably. Legal systems can set conditions as to the character of rules (universality, consistency, etc.) and to the forms of their passing (majorities, 'expert' scrutiny in drafting, etc.). Constitutions, fundamental constitutional laws and rights, supreme or constitutional courts are apparatuses of limitation of legislative and political practice, for example. Legal apparatuses and categories have political and other conditions of existence and effectivity, but within those conditions (however limiting), they constitute a specific sphere of effectivity which synthesises rather than merely reflects the determinations acting on it.[8]

The concept of law-as-origin (whether an origin in social relations or ethical will or juridic creativity) unifies the form of law with a definite content: it imposes the consistency necessary to essence and to a unitary origin. Nothing could be more dangerous to the analysis of legislation and juridic practice. Law is assigned a content it cannot transgress – in the case currently under consideration a particular concept of property right and the subject of right. The effectivity of legal apparatuses is set at zero, they offer no constraints to a content of legality set outside them. Socialists confronting the particular legal-economic forms of modern capitalism, attempting reforms through legislative procedures or defending political practices against the courts can only be blinded and lose by subscribing to an essentialist doctrine of law.

Pashukanis' rejection of the pertinence of legislation in the explanation of law depends on certain theoretical conditions. Accepting this pertinence does not entail falling into the errors of idealist legal philosophy. Idealism is the counterpart and opponent of materialism, but only within a field of discourse. In criticising the concept of social totality on which Pashukanis' materialism depends we have gone beyond this discursive field. Taking the form and determinants of legislation seriously in the analysis of law does not entail spiritualistic premises or explanations. Laws are ascribed not to a spirit or the will of a subject but the action of definite conditions.

The second condition of Pashukanis' separation of the form of law from the general class-coercive functioning of the state is a particular conception of the state itself. We have seen that public law is a derivative juridicalisation of the state, which cloaks in the form of right the actual basis of its operations. In effect while rejecting the class reductionist account of law in general, Pashukanis accepts the vulgar Marxist-Leninist concept of the state as a coercive apparatus in the hands of the exploiting class. The state is an apparatus of repression based on coercive power.

It works through command, non-reciprocal orders which require obedience and are backed by force. The form of law as right is contrasted with state power which works through command, subordination and force.

This difference between the form of law and the state is clearest in Pashukanis' conception of the criminal law. Criminal law is incorporated within the form of law, it adopts the institutional superstructure of legality. Crime in capitalism is conceived on the analogy with private law as the violation by the criminal of a right borne by society, a violation of obligation which requires recompense. But this extension of the legal form is a mere ideological cover:

> The criminal jurisdiction of the bourgeois state is organised class terror, differing only in degree from the so-called extraordinary measures applied to the elements of civil war . . . If the matter is looked at from this point of view, the criminal court is merely an appendage of the machinery made up of the police and the department of investigation.
>
> Pashukanis (p. 212)[9]

The inadequacies of this vulgar Marxist-Leninist concept of state should by now be evident: virtually no school of modern Marxism subscribes to it.[10] It reduces the apparatuses of the state to instruments of coercion and their action to repression. This Marxist double of the 'nightwatchman state' is not a mere product of Pashukanis' left-wing Bolshevik politics. Ascribing complex and 'positive' social functions to the state, assigning it the role of directing and rendering cohesive a variety of ideological means of perpetuation of the dominant social relations (as a host of modern Marxists from 'Althusserians' to Euro-communists to the varied disciples of the ambiguous prophet Gramsci tend to do) blurs the distinction between state and civil society. Pashukanis needs this classic distinction in its sharpest form to differentiate private law and its functions from the state. Private law is an organic product of civil society. This distinction not only involves an inadequate conception of the state – an apparatus of coercion separate from and opposed to the body of the social – but it returns us to the problems discussed under the first condition by conceiving civil society as an homogenous entity with necessary effects.

We must now turn from the theoretical conditions which permit the differentiation of the form of law from the state to Pashukanis' analysis of the genesis of this form. Private law, the law of property in particular, is the foundation of this form. We have seen that the general concept of law is that of a realm of subjects as bearers of right:

> The specific fact distinguishing the legal order from every other social order is that it is based upon private isolated subjects. A norm of law acquires its *differentia specifica* – which distinguishes it from the general mass of governing rules (including moral, aesthetic and utilitarian rules) – by the fact that it presupposes a person endowed with a right and, moreover, actively asserting a claim.
>
> Pashukanis (p. 153)

This general concept entails three elements: (i) the existence of subjects separated one from another – individuated; (ii) the relation between the subject and the right – possession; (iii) the nature of the relation of the subjects one to another and to rights, private-possession, the subjects are separated one from another as possessors and defined by an exclusive relation to right. Private law originates in social relations which have those attributes of individuation – separation, possession-exclusion. Private law is founded on private property. Only private property in the form of *commodities* supports these attributes. Feudal and communal property introduce political or communal relations between subjects and possession, and, moreover link subjects one to another in definite ways.

Law arises as a medium of resolution of disputes between separated individuals over exclusive possession. The possibility of disputes taking a form which is formally resoluble arises because of the characteristics of commodity exchange. Developed commodity exchange takes the form of *equivalence*: labour products are equated in exchange. On the basis of this social form of exchange, juridical conceptions of equity and restitution arise. Exchange is a transfer of equivalent possessions, it involves the obligation of reciprocity. Equivalence is formal not ethical, and concerns a right to a definite quantum. The basic substance of the law, therefore, is a dispute between parties to an exchange or contract involving obligations patterned on it. Legal resolution of the dispute consists in the determination of obligation and the restitution of an amount equivalent to it. This determination is a matter of fact and the amount of restitution is calculable, stemming from the obligation itself. Law, the restoration of equivalents to which right creates an obligation, is thereby differentiated from moralty and command. It is concerned with the *fact* of possession of a right and the corresponding obligation.

Central to Pashukanis' concept of law is the concept of *subject* (see Appendix I). Law is concerned with the relation of subjects one to another in respect of their possession of rights. Private law is the specific form of law (distinguishing legal norms from others) because the subject can pursue his defence of a right (which he 'possesses') as the action of an independent individual (this pursuit is independent of political command or its moral worth). Law is a sphere of inter-subjectivity – it is the interaction of autonomous subjects in pursuit of rights which gives it its substance. The concept of legal subject (the possessor of a right) is a development from the subject of commodity exchange (the possessor of alienable things capable of entering into an exchange of equivalents with another possessor):

> Every sort of juridic relationship is a relationship between subjects. A subject is the atom of juridic theory: the simplest element, incapable of being resolved further . . . it is only as freedom of disposition in the market that property becomes the basis of development of the legal form, and the category 'subject' serves as the best expression of that freedom.
>
> Pashukanis (p. 160)

The basis of the law is the commodity form and the subject corresponding to it.

Pashukanis argues that the economic subject, the individual as possessor, is a direct function of the form of commodity exchange:

> In Marx the analysis of the form of the subject flows directly and immediately out of analysis of the form of the commodity.[11]
>
> Ibid (p. 162)

The commodity form (alienable-equivalent) generates a subject appropriate to it, autonomous individuals possessing alienable things. The form of commodity exchange arises from the conditions of commodity production and the subject it supposes is the product of the production relationships which entail the circulation of the social product in the form of commodities. The individual subject as possessor of alienable things is a function of the separation/alienation of producers one from another in this form of society. The division of social labour takes the form of independent individual producers and the interdependence of the differentiated branches of production. The division of labour makes the individual producers the possessors of their labour products, needing to enter into exchange to secure the means of their livelihood, and confronting other producers in exchange. The social link between men is the circulation of things, the products of their labour. The products of labour are both private possessions and alienable things:

> The social link binding persons in the process of production . . . thus requires for its realisation a special relationship of persons as disposers of products: as subjects 'whose will is dominant over things' . . . At the very same time, therefore, that the product of labour is taking on the quality of goods (commodities) and becoming a bearer of value, man acquires the quality of a juridic subject and becomes the bearer of a right.
>
> Ibid (p. 162)

The subject of law is a direct reflection of the conditions of commodity exchange.

With the full development of generalised commodity production the legal subject takes on its most developed form – subjects become identical and equal. Abstract labour is reflected in the abstraction of legal form: the subjects of right become fully equivalent as possessors, like their labours and their products in the social process of exchange (without economically impertinent differences of status). Pashukanis says:

> Only with the complete development of bourgeois relationships does the law acquire an abstract character. Each man becomes a man in general; labour of every sort is reduced to socially . . . (necessary) . . . labour in general, and every subject becomes an abstract juridic subject.
>
> Ibid (p. 169)

The form of law emerges directly from the commodity form: it is an effect of the social relations of commodity production. The legal subject and property right are extensions of the economic subjects necessary to commodity production: independent/interdependent individuals who possess alienable things. This economic subject is a necessary effect of the social process whereby economic relations 'represent' themselves in their subjective conditions. Pashukanis is committed by this logic to the identification of the essential form of capitalist property with individual private property managed in the social process of production by the possessing subject.

Corporate forms of capital are inassimilable to this coincidence of subjects (owning, possessing, calculating). Monopoly, in separating ownership and possession, legal subject and economic subject, dissolves the connections which are necessary to capitalist social relations proper:

> As the capitalist means of production develop, the property owner is gradually liberated from the technical functions of production, while at the same time he loses as well the

completeness of juridic dominance of his capital. In an enterprise represented by shares of stock, the individual capitalist is merely the bearer of a title to a certain proportion of non-labour income. His economic and juridic activity as a property owner is confined exclusively to the sphere of a nonproductive consumer. The basic mass of capital becomes in full measure an impersonal class force . . . In reality . . . (capital) . . . is managed by a relatively small handful of the biggest capitalists which acts, moreover, through its hired representatives and agents. A juridically distinct form of private property no longer reflects the true state of things for the reason that . . . the factual dominance extends far beyond the purely juridic framework.

(p. 176)

The consequences of this development are as follows:

   (i) the subject of property right as mere shareholder ceases to be an economic subject, he becomes the holder of a pure and functionless title to a portion of the surplus-value;
   (ii) capitalists as economic subjects remain, they annex lesser capitals to their own management;
   (iii) capital becomes an impersonal (depersonified) class force;
   (iv) individual private property no longer reflects the actual socialised character of production.

Pashukanis, far from recognising the corporate enterprise as a new form of effective possession and management of capital thus conceives 'monopoly' capital as the reign of a few super-capitalists and as the sphere of action of the increasingly depersonified total social capital (its movements no longer even take the phenomenal form of the results of human wills). Monopoly is a transitional form, the sign of the redundancy and impending dissolution of capitalist social and property relations: 'Here we approach the moment when capitalist society has already sufficiently matured to pass into its opposite'. Ibid (p.

176). Pashukanis argues that the general form of law will cease to exist with the disappearance of its material substratum, the commodity form: 'The dying out of the categories of bourgeois law will in these conditions signify the dying out of law in general: that is to say, the gradual disappearance of the juridic element in human relations'. Ibid (p. 122).

Law is based on the law of value: the relation of equivalence between commodities is the foundation of the specificity of the legal norm as against other norms. Thus in a communist society with the supersession of the law of value there is a supersession of the form of law: all legal forms are *bourgeois*, the notion of a 'proletarian law' is a pernicious absurdity. The legal form will remain under a socialist regime only during that transitional period during which, as Marx argues in *The Critique of the Gotha Programme*, the necessity of the proportionality of rewards to labour time remains.[12]   With the end of the relation of equivalence there ends the form of law.

In the late twenties and early thirties Pashukanis' school occupied a prominent position in Soviet jurisprudence and conducted an extensive campaign to get their conceptions of the 'withering away of law' put into effect. With the attenuation of the community form the objective need for law disappears: revolutionary jurists should take the lead in promoting this process. Legal codes should be progressively simplified and should inceasingly record objective states of affairs rather than refer to subjective categories like norms, intentions, responsibilities, etc. Codes would eventually be replaced by administrative rulings in particular cases, decisions adjusted to 'soviet reality', and by the decisions of 'comrades courts' in questions of personal conduct, decisions based on an overall political judgement of the individual rather than the application of a norm. The penal measures of criminal law would be replaced by measures of 'social defence' which controlled and adapted behaviour to the forms required by Soviet life. This campaign to abolish legal forms was brought to an end by the consolidation of Stalin's rule, the intensification of the purges and the justification of the terror as the application of 'Soviet socialist law'. Vyshinskii's con-

ception of law, which now became dominant, restored the notion
of law as norm and the specificity of the legal process which
Pashukanis' had challenged in his earlier work (needless to say,
Vyshinskii travestied this notion of socialist legality in his practice
as prosecutor in the more notorious of the treason trials).

B *Renner*

Karl Renner's *Institutions of Private Law and their Social Functions* is
justly regarded as *the* classic Marxist text on the law of property.
Its methodology in respect of law is, however, not drawn like
Pashukanis' from the general body of Marxist theory. Renner
adopted the formalist legal philosophy dominant in central
Europe at the time. Renner's formalism is not a mere matter of
intellectual 'influences' for it was put to work in the body of his
Marxism. Renner uses the formalist thesis about the autonomy of
legal concepts to attempt the same operation which Pashukanis
accomplishes by drawing on Marx's insistence on the explanation of the *form* of value, that is, the liberation of the analysis of
legal forms and institutions forms a simple and immediate
reduction to economic 'interests' and forces. The thesis of
autonomy enables Renner to treat the institutions of private law
as an independent *legal totality*, recognising the specific legality of
their interrelations rather than reducing them term by term to
the economic facts they reflect.

Renner separates the form of legal institutions from the social
functions which they perform. The social functions of the law
may change radically whilst the legal institutions and concepts
remain relatively constant. Legal categories and legal practice
and its social effects do not correspond. The determinants of the
social functions the law performs are beyond legal institutions
themselves. Analysis of institutional form and social function
must be separated.

Renner argues that legal institutions are combined in specific
ways (determined by the social relations) to serve economic
processes: capitalist production, for example, a single economic
category, requires the legal categories of exercise of a right

(capitalist as property holder) and fulfillment of a contractual obligation (worker as seller of labour power). Renner remarks:

> Thus a simple economic category is equivalent to a combination of various legal categories, there is no point-to-point correspondence. A number of distinct legal institutions serves a single economic process. They play a part which I will call their economic function.
>
> Renner (p. 57)

The economic function is that of support as mediator of a process. Legal institutions serve a *social* function to the extent that the economic process supported is part of the whole process of production and reproduction. These 'social functions' are those which facilitate reproduction and, therefore, the maintenance of 'society' as a whole.

Renner adopts the Austro-Marxist conception of 'society', a view he shares with the noted economist Rudolf Hilferding.[13] Society is an association of individuals. Thus, for Renner, law is a relation of control between individuals; legal corporations are 'fictious' for definite human subjectivities. Despite this apparent methodological individualism 'society' is constantly conceived as an entity with needs which must be realised in the actions of individuals. The mechanisms by which these social ends are met vary: in commodity production it is as the unconscious result of numerous individual actions, a result secured by the law of value which governs these acts; in socialism it is by means of conscious collective direction. Social functions are connected with social needs, the process of reproduction secures the material conditions of social life:

> The regulation of labour and goods determines the legal form of the process of preservation of the species, since it regulates the power of disposal over labour and means of production.
>
> Renner (p. 74)

Renner begins his analysis of how legal institutions serve to support essential economic functions by considering the social relations of simple commodity production. Here the institutions of private law *correspond* to the categories of economy:

> We start with the historical beginnings of the institution, with the period of simple commodity production, the initial stage of bourgeois society. *For there is always a moment* in the history of human institutions when the legal system is an adequate expression of economic relations, when superstructure and substructure are in conformity.
>
> Renner (p. 83)

Having postulated non-correspondence in general, Renner goes on to establish a direct correspondence between the economy and its legal expression-form. Non-correspondence is produced by the advent of capitalism and its evolution, until it creates the conditions for a new correspondence between consciously constructed socialist legal forms and a planned economy. Renner merely refuses the constant and immediate correspondence of legal institutions and economic forms, he does not cease to make legal institutions a direct expression of economic needs.

In simple commodity production there is a correspondence of property law and the whole social process of production: the right of detention serves all the social functions of reproduction. Society is divided into household units of production and consumption linked with one another through the market. The possessor (of his labour product and its equivalent in exchange) is in a position to regulate the orders of both labour (production) and consumption through the goods he owns. The doctrine of absolute property right of an individual over 'things' is adequate to social relations in which men as independent producers are connected simply through the exchange of their products.[14] The possession of *things* is therefore the possession of the social conditions of reproduction. (Labour does not take a social form except through the exchange of its products, the possessing subject is also *by nature* possessor of his own labour power.) Law here regulates *possession* and disputes concerning it. Definition and adjudication of *property* relations is sufficient for all *economic* relations.

Renner goes on to consider transformation in the social functions of legal institutions created by the advent of capitalism. Capitalism separates the worker from the means of production; as a consequence property right becomes no longer sufficient to provide all the conditions of reproduction. The function of detention does not bring with it control over the order of labour. Labour is now separated from the unit of production and the property form. It must be combined with the means of production through a distinct legal institution, that of contract and the obligations arising from it.

Renner analyses the effects of the concentration and centralisation of capital and the development of finance capital on capitalist property relations. As in *Capital* he conceives the joint-stock company as an index of the fact that capitalist property relations have become superfluous as relations of production, they have become an obstacle to the socialised character of production and have no part in the production process. Renner argues, following *Capital*, that the shareholder ceases to have possession of the means of production through property right, ownership becomes a mere title to a portion of the surplus value:

> by the development of interest – bearing capital to an organised credit system and that of corporate associations, the owner is rendered completely superfluous.
>
> Renner (p. 146)

The capitalist is transformed into a mere finance-capitalist, a rentier. He ceases even to administer his capital *as capital* and is replaced by paid functionaries:

The finance capitalist no longer administers his capital for himself, nor does he even lend it himself, for he deposits it in banks or invests it in joint-stock companies and the like. Every function is carried out by persons in salaried positions.

Ibid.

This superfluity of the capitalist in production is fated 'to bring about the self-abolition of property even within a capitalist system of production, for even to the law the owner is either no longer owner or merely one of a multitude of owners without influence'. Renner (p. 220)[15]

As the capitalists' right of property ceases to support positive social functions so economic roles and the social functions of legal institutions change. The manager of the productive enterprise, a salaried functionary, takes over the functions of organisation and control of production hitherto performed by the capitalist as a consequence of his possession of the means of productions. The legal institution corresponding to this economic role is that of the contract of employment which ' . . . takes over the last remaining function of general service to the community as a whole, of those fulfilled by the institution of property'. Renner (p. 200)

For Renner the manager is identified as a socially useful functionary expressing a neutral special skill (which Renner, p. 143, calls a 'gift'). Private property is irrelevant to the enterprise as productive unit. It follows, therefore, that a change in the *form* of property will bring the institutions of property sanctioned by law into correspondence with the, already socialised, conditions of production. The organisation of labour and production is already adequate to socialism.[16]

Renner sums up his conception of the position of the joint-stock company (corporation) in capitalism thus:

> This previously insignificant legal institution has thus deprived property of all functions connected with social production and reproduction, making property itself an inoperative and anti-social institution, to which only one function is left, that of obstructing the future development of society.
>
> Renner (p. 220)

The joint stock company or corporation is central in this degeneration of the organising functions of private property in capitalism. The dominance of this form of capital shows that socialism is both possible and necessary.

3　MARX AND THE JOINT-STOCK COMPANY

At the cost of some repetition we will now consider Marx's conception of the corporate organisation of capital and its effects. This is necessary to convince the sceptic that neither Pashukanis nor Renner is in fact departing from or misreading *Capital*. It is also necessary because Marx's views contradict a great deal of the 'Marxist' and socialist contribution to the debate on ownership and control, which has sought to convince us that the old-time capitalist is alive and well and living in the boardroom.

For Marx the development of the joint-stock company and the creation of a credit system are effects of the concentration and centralisation of capital and the increasingly socialised character of the productive forces. These institutions reflect and accentuate the developing contradiction in the capitalist mode of production between the social character of the productive forces and the ownership of the means of production in the form of private property. This form ceases to be attached to the organising functions in the process of production: the owner of capital as property cedes his functions as possessing subject and subject of economic calculation to managerial functionaries. Property right increasingly ceases to express a functioning *relation of production* and becomes a survival, a mere right to the appropriation of the social product. Capital has moved into the era of irreconcilable contradiction and collapse. Ownership of capital has become a purely parasitic relation and one which now carries the anarchy and irrationality of capitalist production to its limit: 'It is private production without the control of private property' (*Capital* III: p. 429). The limits of scale and on reckless speculation imposed by the fusion of the owning subject and the economic subject, a capitalist dependent on property in the form of a productive enterprise managed by him for his livelihood, are overcome. The owner of capital becomes a *rentier* who is neither limited by the knowledge and experience of a definite line of business nor constrained by the capital market, for a condition of existence of the rentier is the stock-market and the credit system. Capital becomes a mobile force as it has never been before, financial markets are the sphere of speculative irrationality par excellence. The controller of centralised credit, the promoter of shares, make profits from speculative dealings in other's capitals. The socialisation of the *forces* of production, reflected in the concentration and centralisation of capitals, is accompanied by anarchic relations of production dominated by financial capital, speculators and swindlers. Planned production becomes a necessity, a relation of production appropriate to the socialised forces:

> This is the abolition of the capitalist mode of production within the capitalist mode of production itself, and hence a self-dissolving contradiction, which *prima facie* represents a mere phase of transition to a new mode of production.
>
> *Capital* III (p. 429)

The joint-stock company is a sign of a whole social process of contradiction. Its form and consequences can be summed up as follows:

(1) *At the level of the unit of production*, the conversion of the owner into a functionless *rentier* and the adoption of the economic functions of the capitalist by 'a mere manager, administrator of other people's capital' (III: p. 427). Apart from the increasing scale and co-operative nature of the productive process itself nothing more is said about the joint-stock company as a *form of organisation of capital*, as a type of enterprise. This is because capital becomes irrelevant to production as production; the scale and nature of production operations are an effect of the process of development of the forces of production (which ultimately is independent of the particular production relations involved). Capital's relation to production becomes an external, antagonistic and purely appropriative one: it is in contradiction with the forces, an 'antithesis as another's property to every individual actually at work in production, from the manager down to the last day labourer' (III: pp. 427–8). The actual organisation of production lies on the other side of this contradiction, it is an anticipation of and requires socialism. It follows that to talk

about the effects of corporate forms as organisations *of* production is impertinent.

(2) *At the level of the total social capital*, the increasing anarchy of the process of production and distribution. This is promoted by the purely appropriative character of capital and by the forms of social organisation it takes. The stock market and the credit system centralise capital into the hands of a handful of finance capitalist speculators. The owner is appropriated as capitalist and converted into a mere coupon-clipper, parasitically dependent on a process in which he or she plays no part. Capitalism does the preliminary work of socialism 'in a contradictory form, as the appropriation of social property by a few' (III: p. 430). These few have 'more and more the aspect of pure adventures' (p. 430): finance capital is conceived by Marx as taking the form of *individuals*. That is, individual economic subjects who use the capital of others to enrich themselves 'without the control of private property'. Their action is thus unrestrained and inevitably speculative; the centralisation of credit and the control of enterprises in financial markets is the condition and field of action of this speculation.

Financial markets are relatively autonomous from production, the forces of production are here subject to purely financial considerations and calculations of return. The financial capitalist calculates without direct reference to the needs of production. Capital as an economic subject becomes indifferent to its material conditions of existence.

If we consider Marx's argument at the level of the unit of production it bears a striking similarity to that of Berle and Means.[17] The joint-stock company effects a divorce of ownership and control at the level of the unit of production. The owner of capital becomes 'a mere owner, a mere money capitalist' (III: p. 427) and is replaced in the direction of production by the paid functionary. Ownership and control are regarded here solely from the standpoint of their fusion in the person of the industrialist capitalist. Capital is now separated from the actual tasks of management: '. . . profit is henceforth received only in the form of interest, i.e. as a mere compensation for owning capital that is now entirely divorced from the function in the actual process of reproduction' (III: p. 427). The separation Berle and Means argue for is also to be found in Marx. Whereas Berle and Means argue that this can liberate management from the narrow pursuit of profit maximisation to become representatives of 'society' and to take account of wider social interests and goals, Marx argues that the paid functionaries are subordinated to an increasingly irrational social process dominated by finance capital. Berle and Means conceive the enterprise represented by its managers as a subject capable of constituting its effects, capable of persuing its own goals. Economic relations are made the resultant of decisions and actions at enterprise level. Enterprises can decide to pursue goals which are socially rational and need not engage in the naked competition for maximum profit. This conception of enterprise is a variant of the rationalist conception of action,[18] it sets the effect of *forms of relation between enterprises* at nought (or rather as mere effects of their wills). Berle and Means simply follow here the neo-classical concept of economic subject, attaching to it the attributes of representative of society and of *social* rationality. In this concept economic forms are nothing but inter-subjectivity and its effects (markets prices distribution effects, etc.).[19]

Marx correctly opposes such a conception, insisting on the effectivity of economic forms as forms. His rejection and critique of this form of the rationalist conception of action in political economy is one of his greatest theoretical achievements. This avoidance is won at a (very high) price. Marx conceives enterprises and individual capitals as mere fragments of the totality of capital in motion. Capitals are part of a totality which internalises its effects, as such they can have no effective autonomy in relation to the realisation of those effects. Marx's concept of the economic subject is that of representative of the totality, the subject receives the content of economic calculation and its grounds of action from the necessary social process of representation. This, as we have seen, requires individual subjects endowed with the faculty of experience. Marx's universal subject is different from neo-classicism's (it is not constitutive), but as such, as a universal subject it produces curiously parallel effects. Marx's conception of the joint-stock company as 'private production without the control of private property' resembles conservative capitalist arguments against the large-scale corporate enterprise. Aside from the danger of monopoly and the distributive virtues of competition there is in the anti-corporatist argument the notion of the *discipline* imposed by the correspondence of ownership and management. Here is an example of reactionary thundering from the *Law Times*:

> There is an abundance of capital in this country. We are the lenders of our surplus capital to every nation in the world. Any sudden demand, any new opening for speculation is at once supplied with inexhaustible funds, while we are subject to the frequent recurrence of periods of undue and dangerous inflation of credit and speculation. When these periods occur the tendency of the measure must be to extend and intensify these evils by giving facility for the widespread introduction of joint-stock companies, reckless in their procedure because protected by limited liability and filling the community with instruments of gambling in the form of shares upon which little or nothing has been paid up.
>
> Lords Overstone and Monteagle, *Law Times* 21 June 1856

Marx resembles this ultraism ('speculators', 'adventurers', 'parasites', etc.) because for him the carrier of capitalist social relations (as production relations) is the individual capitalist. The capitalist is limited in his actions by the coincidence of ownership possession and calculation: his experience of the social process of capital forces him to attend in some measure to the realities of production; the experience of the *rentier* and finance capitalist, insulated in the financial sphere, does not.

My co-authors and I have discussed the limits of Marx's conception of the enterprise in capitalism in some detail in *Marx's Capital and Capitalism Today*. I will briefly review the points which are pertinent here. Firstly, Marx systematically confuses capital as a social relation with particular rights of private property. The unit of possession of capital (means of production) in the case under consideration is the corporate enterprise itself. This form of possession makes possible, and exists because of, a transformation in the scale of funds necessary for certain branches of production and types of enterprise. The shares are not as such capital in this sense, only pooled and combined in one unit of possession do they function as capital (as means of production). This unit of possession must be directed as a single economic agency. Effective possession of capital and the functions of economic calculation are *combined* in the form of the corporate enterprise.[2(] It is only because Marx identifies the owners of shares as *capitalists* that he can argue as he does about the separation of ownership and management, whereas what is at stake is the combination of effective possession and an appropriate organisational form of economic calculation.

Marx fails to analyse the share as a legal-economic form. Here I will presume British institutions since the Companies Act of 1862 (the specific legal form is important and affects the conditions of organisation and operation of capitalist enterprises – Marx pays no attention to it or to possible variations in this form). Equity shares are a marketable financial asset with a (variable) dividend yield and attached to which are certain rights (which vary between classes of share and companies), rights of participation in the governance of the company concerned. Shares are alienable to the extent that a market for them exists, this depends on the status (whether quoted or unquoted) and the performance of the company and on the state of the general market. A sale represents a mere *transfer* of the rights in question. The capital of a company is unaffected by such transfers. The seller receives a money price for a title, he does not dispose of the company's assets. Shares become a means of effective possession of the assets of a company to the holder only if he or she has control over a majority of the voting shares (this control is, in law, subject to the rights of other shareholders to dividend, maintenance of capital, etc.). In the absence of this condition effective possession is vested in a board of directors who are 'representatives' of the shareholders and the managements appointed by them. The company is a legal entity separate from its shareholders and can only be dissolved by a majority agreeing to a motion for winding-up.[21]

This is the formal organisational-legal position. In practice company organisation bears little relation to this notion of a republic of shareholders governed by their elected representatives. Most large companies are run by a self-replacing professional management and directorate whose policies and nominations receive formal assent at shareholders' meetings. Marx identifies the shareholder with the *rentier* owner of capital. We have challenged the notion that it is necessarily *capital* which is owned in the form of the share, now we will go on to challenge the notion that the shareholder is a parasitic *rentier*. There is no necessary or archetypical 'shareholder', whether it be the bloated coupon-clipper or the famous widows and orphans of Wall Street apologetics. Precisely because shares are marketable assets patterns of share ownership can change with changing economic circumstances and the types of economic agents entering into the stock market. Shares in quoted companies are *increasingly held by financial institutions and other companies*. A glance at Tables 1 and 2 (Tables 9 and 10 from the report of the Royal Commission on the Distribution of Income and Wealth) will confirm this. In 1973 financial institutions, companies and public bodies held over 52 per cent of quoted ordinary shares (5 per cent being held by overseas investors and 42 per cent by persons, executors and trustees), the total held by financial institutions was 38.3 per cent. The proportion of shares held by the institutions has been rising steadily in recent years, as a glance at Table 2 will indicate.[22]

Financial institutions and companies can function in relation to the enterprises whose shares they purchase in two primary ways, either as investment banks or holding companies (whether formally or *de facto*), acquiring a substantial portion of the equity and more or less closely directing company policy, or as portfolio holders on a large scale, spreading risks and oriented primarily to stock market values and dividend yields. There is no necessary pattern of consequences which follows from institutional shareownership, company managements will encounter very

TABLE 1 The pattern of ownership of quoted ordinary shares in UK companies 31 December 1973

Category of ownership	Market value of ordinary shares held £ million	Percentage of total ordinary shares in issue %
1. Persons, executors and trustees resident in UK	17,010	42.0
2. Charities and other non-profit making bodies	1,780	4.4
3. Insurance companies		
– long term funds	5,760	14.2
– general funds	790	2.0
4. Pension funds	4,950	12.2
5. Investment trust companies	2,640	6.5
6. Unit trusts	1,390	3.4
7. Banks and other financial institutions	1,340	3.3
8. Non-financial companies	1,730	4.3
9. Public sector	1,020	2.5
10. Overseas	2,110	5.2
11. Total	40,520	100

Source: 1. Inland Revenue Statistics (HMSO).   2. CSO.

Table 2 The pattern of owership of quoted ordinary shares 1963 and 1969–73

Category of ownership	1963	1969	1970	1971	1972	1973
						Percentage (year-end)
Persons, executors and trustees resident in UK	58.7	47.0	45.0	44.0	43.0	42.0
Charities and other non-profit making bodies	2.6	3.6	3.8	4.0	4.2	4.4
Insurance companies						
– long term funds	10.6	12.4	13.0	13.7	13.8	14.2
– general funds		1.4	1.4	1.6	1.7	2.0
Pension funds	7.0	9.4	10.4	11.0	11.3	12.2
Investment trust companies	6.7	7.0	6.9	7.0	6.9	6.5
Unit trusts	1.2	2.9	2.9	3.2	3.1	3.4
Banks and other financial institutions	2.3	3.6	3.7	3.5	3.7	3.3
Non-financial companies	4.8	4.6	4.7	4.6	4.7	4.3
Public sector	1.6	2.5	2.4	1.8	1.9	2.5
Overseas	4.4	5.6	5.8	5.6	5.7	5.2
Total	100	100	100	100	100	100
Total market value of issued ordinary shares (£ million)	27,500	38,010	35,670	50,920	60,070	40,520

Source: Diamond Commission Report No. 2, Tables 9 and 10 (1975), p. 17.

different regimes depending on the circumstances. What this trend in shareownership does show is that Marx fails to consider that there are other supports for corporate capitalist organisation than a *lumpencapitalist rentier* class. Capital can be generated through the sale of insurance policies, through pension schemes, and the concentration of the bank deposits of wage earners and enterprises. The institutions involved purchase shares on the basis of these funds. These shares represent capital, means of production, to the enterprises selling them. They represent financial capital in the form of shares to the institutions, simultaneously a means of meeting their commitments and making profits. They do not represent capital to the persons who buy insurance or bank their wages. What the customers of these institutions possess is titles to interest, right to money sums in certain circumstances, etc., not capital.

Moreover, the sale of equities is no longer the major means of company finance in this country. Financial institutions of necessity trade primarily in the secondary market in existing equities. Since the 1950s internally generated funds (retained profit, depreciation) have on average contributed about 75 per cent of investment, bonds 11 per cent, bank borrowing 6 per cent, and shares proper a mere 7 per cent (moreover, the proportion of bank loans to equity has tended to increase).[23] The *rentier*, even if he were the archetypical shareholder, would be marginal to the actual sources of capitalist finance.

Capital is a social relation of production, a relation based upon the construction of an exclusive possession of the means of production by economic agents in the form of enterprises which produce commodities by wage labour in order to obtain profit. Social relations of production effecting this separation from the means of production of the mass of the working people can exist without the personification of this exclusive possession in the form of individual private property. Capitalism is a system of production in which considerations of profit and the requirements of forms of exclusive possession predominantly determine what is produced. The joint-stock company did not alter this fact, it neither represents a sign of the dissolution of capitalist relations of

production nor the advent of 'social responsibility' in commodity
production.

Let us turn from the industrial capitalist joint-stock enterprise
to the financial system in which it operates. Marx, as we have
seen, considers the stock-market and the credit system as
essentially speculative forms controlled by a handful of adventurers. It would be idle to deny the existence of speculators and
adventurers, equally it would be a serious error to overrate their
importance. The centralisation of financial markets and the
credit system has led to the domination of corporate enterprises,
banks and other institutions, holding companies, etc., not
individual super-capitalist adventurers. Indeed, it is those
institutions which are the main *means* of centralisation. Institutions have economic conditions of existence which limit their
operations, pensions funds and insurance companies have calculable and regular payments to meet from returns on invested
funds, banks have deposits subject to immediate withdrawal, etc.
In consequence they cannot in general operate like adventurers
or swindlers, notorious instances apart. This does not imply that
the institutions have made capitalism a stable and rational
economic system, far from it,[24] but the forms of speculation
'without the control of private property' Marx envisages have
always been scandals which rock the stock market and the credit
system rather than the dominant and normal forms of its
operation.

4   WHY THE LEGAL FORM OF CORPORATE PROPERTY IS POLITICALLY IMPORTANT

The pertinences of the arguments advanced above are not
confined to showing the *theoretical* limitations of the classical
Marxist treatments of the corporation. This weakness has been
coupled with a political passivity in regard to questions of the
organisation of capital. Marxists have treated the form of organisation as necessarily given in the system of production and so
have neglected debates and struggles concerning the legal

regulation and economic organisation of capital as objects of political struggle. Marxists have classically considered law as being merely the juridical expression of the actual relations of production and that these relations are given in their form by the structure of the mode of production. I have argued at length here and elsewhere that the relations of production cannot be held to secure their own conditions of existence without the introduction of the problematic concept of a totality which internalises its effects. Once this concept is abandoned then it follows that the mode in which the conditions of operation of capitalist relations of production are secured can vary and that these variations in mode affect the operations of those relations. This is particularly clear in the case of the law of property and company law and questions of capitalist organisation.

The problem of what a 'capital' is cannot be separated from questions of the legal definition of its form of organisation. There is no given form of this organisation. The classical Marxist concept of 'capitalist' and the modern Roman Law conception of the subject of property right as a natural person endowed with rights of detention and alienation of things do indeed correspond in large measure. This is a correspondence which derives from the particular political-legal conditions of the development of capitalism in continental Europe and not from the nature of capitalism itself. The creation of modern corporate forms of property required changes in the law. These legal changes were necessary in order that the various forms of modern corporate organisation could become possible but they did not necessitate them – the legal institutions and the forms of economic organisation are relatively separate and have distinct determinants.

I will attempt to illustrate these remarks by referring to the development of incorporation and limited liability in this country in the course of the last century.[25] Marxists have tended to treat the development of limited liabiliy simply as a function of the development of the forces of production and the forms of concentration of capital required by them. This legal form then appears as a necessary 'expression' of the objective developments in capitalist production. Such an analysis is naively apolitical:

law becomes an 'expression', a recognition of what is, rather than an arena of struggle, a form with potential political and economic effects.

The struggle for the general availability of incorporation and for limited liability was a complex contest of distinct political and economic forces with various public policy objectives and economic interests. One thing is certain – industrial capital and the production of manufactured commodities is marginal to it. In order to comprehend the nature of the struggle for incorporation and limited liability it is necessary to begin with the legal conditions against which it was directed. The Bubble Act of 1720 was an emergency measure introduced as a result of the financial crisis caused by the difficulties of the South Sea Company. The Act, a panic measure, was poorly drafted and sweeping in effect, making all economic combinations (other than partnerships or having a Royal Charter or being incorporated by Act of Parliament) illegal. In large measure it was an attempt to bolster the privileges of the ailing Company (and thereby secure the redemption of the public debt which was one of the objectives of the South Sea scheme) and challenge the speculation fuelled by the promotion of parallel schemes. This self-interested panic measure by the government became in the subsequent struggles and debates identified as the cornerstone of a public policy of financial regulation. According to this position prescription of combination and unlimited liability would constrain, by the very risks involved, speculative financial promotions. It served, it was claimed, thereby to protect creditors, to protect the investor against his own gullibility and to ensure stability in the loan and credit markets. This policy sought (and failed) to prevent speculative financial crises and the disruption of trade by hitting at what were thought to be the organisational forms which promoted speculation (individual trading and unlimited liability – 'the control of private property' with a vengeance – would make the risks involved unacceptable).

The 1720 Act was hardly a successful measure of financial regulation but to call it as Formoy[26] does 'merely a dead letter' is to miss the point. The full development of the joint-stock company required *positive* legislation. The absence of sanctioned and regulated rights for investors which followed from the Act of 1720 was a constraint in itself to many categories of enterprise and investor but not to speculative promoters and unthinking investors. The same situation was perpetuated after the repeal of the Act in 1825 (acting as a corporate body was not an offence in Common Law independent of statute, companies without public recognition now came exclusively under the Common Law), it was the absence of legal definition and protection of investors' rights which acted as a constraint and the absence of prescription did not remedy this.

Between the early 1800s and 1844 there was a period of intense debate and struggle over what policy objectives were to be pursued and whose rights were to be sanctioned in company law. In this period investors were at the mercy of speculative projectors acting within the existing forms of law (and the absence of disclosure, registration and regulation which they involved). The Report of the Select Committee on Joint-Stock Companies 1844 represents a decisive switch in the conception of public policy and its objectives. Official opinion switched from prohibition and the punishment of offenders as a means to correct speculation and fraud to legal regulation and disclosure, and it switched from a primary concern for the rights of the creditor to a recognition of the need to protect the investor.[27] The succession of Acts between 1844 and 1862 was primarily devised to protect the investor and to secure the integrity of the invested capital. They were in large measure a by-product of the 'unacceptable face' of the railway and mining share booms and the mushrooming of private banks. But in no sense were they made *necessary* by the forms of economic organisation of production and finance then dominant. Individual possession, partnership and mortgage were adequate organisational forms for industrial capital. Institutions like Lloyds and the private unincorporated banks demonstrate the capacity to organise complex financial enterprises without the joint-stock legal form. The *Circular to Bankers* (6 November 1885) remarked:

The Railways system advanced and became established in the public confidence almost wholly without the assistance of the Stock Exchange. The support afforded to it was derived almost exclusively from the capitalists and men of thrift and opulence in the manufacturing and mining districts of the north of England.[28]

The mines and railways did not require the joint-stock or corporate form as units of production. Most mines were technically primitive and in terms of necessary working capital many mining companies were grossly oversubscribed.[29] Mines and railways served as means of financial promotion, they were the objective pretexts of a financial and credit system developed far beyond the needs or organisation of manufacturing enterprises proper. The share booms must be explained in terms of the development of commerce, banking and finance, not in terms of production technique or scale. Indeed, a striking fact about the financial structure is its relative *divorce* from industry – financial and stock market crises and trade crises have a quite separate temporality and set of determinants in this period.

B. C. Hunt's *The Development of the Business Corporation in England 1800–1867* documents these circumstances admirably. He shows that the companies incorporated and the sections of capital pushing for generally available incorporation were public utilities (docks, canals, water undertakings, etc.),[30] banking, insurance and other financial capital. He also argues that limited liability was introduced to protect the investor from the effects of speculative promotions and not because of any shortage of capital for investment.[31] Manufacturing capital did not press for and did not utilise limited liability forms to any extent before 1862 and only on an extensive scale sometime thereafter (the 1880s):

> In those branches of industry really representative of the industrial revolution – the making of cloth, metal-working and mining – joint-stock enterprise was of minor importance until much later in the century.
>
> Hunt (p. 16)

The political struggles and legal measures in no sense *followed* the course of concentration in manufacturing enterprise. Indeed, it can be argued that the legal recognition of the joint-stock/limited liability form of organisation created certain of the organisational conditions of existence for the foundation of large new firms and the mergers of others in the 1880s and 90s. The development of capitalist enterprises using the legal framework of the joint-stock company has not been bound by the circumstances determining its introduction or by the policy objectives of its projectors and proponents. The Act of 1862 gave substantial freedom of action to companies in the matter of internal organisation, an explicit consideration of public policy being *not* to intervene in questions of economic management as far as possible and to avoid 'restraint of trade' by prescribing organisational forms of capital through the law.[32] Companies have taken full advantage of this legalised latitude. It must also be stressed that the company form has been by no means confined to large enterprises raising capital on a stock exchange: many different types of enterprise from the small independent trader adopting the company form to the large multi-divisional group of companies utilise the same basic legal institutions. Perhaps it is this institutionalised latitude which has helped to produce the 'invisibility' of the legal conditions of capitalist organisation to the left in this country and to a consistent underrating of legal regulation through company organisation.

This is *par excellence* the area in which the 'productionism' of classical Marxism has blinded it to the reality of the political struggles involved in the legal regulation of the organisation of capital and in the definition of property right. Marx was fully aware of the role played by legal regulation in questions of the working day, factory conditions and combinations of workers. In *Capital* the length of the working day, working conditions and the level of money wages are *not* given by the structure of the capitalist mode of production and are the subject of class struggle and determined by it. As we have seen Marx allows no such flexibility to questions of the organisation of capital. Yet these questions were the subject of extended and serious struggle *within* the propertied classes in the nineteenth century, a struggle which left its traces in the economic literature, in the courts and in government reports. Marx, an intelligent user of the materials given in evidence in government reports, is largely silent on these documents – particularly the Report of 1844.[33] He recognises the speculation but ignores the discussion of ways of countering it.

Companies Acts are not merely a matter for capitalists or a *fait accompli* enforced by the level of development of the forces of production. In the nineteenth century the political struggles concerned the rights of the investor to protection from fraud and bankruptcy, a matter of concern for the wealthy and the well-to-do. Questions of company law and organisation now concern the rights of the working people, in particular, to avoid the fate of the enterprises in which they work being decided over their heads. I mentioned earlier that the conception of the joint-stock company as a republic of shareholders was largely a fiction. The 'shareholder' is increasingly a financial institution or holding company (mergers and group structures mean that most workers in large-scale enterprises are employees of subsidiary companies). The share is a marketable financial asset to which are attached certain rights of participation in the governance of the company; his means that the stock market is potentially a market in the control of companies. Although share issues are a declining source of investment capital, the fact that companies are organised as joint-stock companies subject to the governance of those appointed by a majority of shareholders has its effects. The stock exchange is both a source of potential control of a company and a measure of its performance (the value of its quotation) which management cannot afford to ignore. This is not to argue existing managements are always efficient and enlightened, never-the-less, in the last twenty years or so the merger boom, the activities of 'asset-strippers', and 'rationalisation' in the interests of one or two of the dominant companies in an industry – all engineered or made possible by the quotation of companies on the stock market – indicate that the working people have plenty to fear from the way capital is organised.[34] A change in the legal form restricting shareholders' rights of control would not eliminate merger, closure or unemployment. It *would* at least eliminate mergers and acquisitions which are resisted by the management of one of the companies involved and restrain the operations of companies whose performance and profits is largely determined by acquiring others. To object by saying that such speculation is the necessary accompaniment of corporate enterprise and the stock market as demonstrated by Marx would be unnecessarily parochial: in Japan for example the stock exchange is relatively undeveloped and does not function as a medium of company acquisition.[35]

Reforms in company law which converted the share into what it is in fact for the individual small investor – a marketable financial asset with a yield but no rights in respect of the governance of a company – would restrict the stock market as a source of company control. It would remain a source of company finance and a market in financial assets – continuing to be patronised by the institutions for that reason. What is the nature of companies as property in that case? A possibility is a form of trust with a self-renewing board of management representing various interests (particularly the employees).[36] These discussions may be dismissed as politically irrelevant speculation. They are irrelevant to the extent that the political leadership of the Labour Movement have made them so. The UCS, 'Work-in' and the Meriden co-operative have demonstrated the willingness of the workers themselves to respond to questions of company closure with innovations in company organisation: a clear legal option in company law for the workers to run a company as a co-operative in a case of failure would have been a real asset in both cases. The Bullock Report, whatever its limits, would have entailed substantial changes in company law. Rather than press for more radical proposals (like a trust with majority representation for the employees on the board of management) the bulk of the Left opposed workers' representation root and branch. In particular they were silent on the prospects the Bullock proposals offered for a thorough debate on company organisation and company law. The points made here are intended to be illustrative, no thorough discussion of company law reform or company organisation can be attempted within the limits of this essay and to do so would direct attention from its primarily theoretical focus. The points at stake here are that company law and organisation does vary, that its forms do matter to the working people and that the Marxist left has immobilised itself by its own indifference and silence.

One word of caution ought to be offered in conclusion to this discussion of reform. Changing company law to restrict shareholders' rights is in no sense a 'socialist' measure *per se*, any more than creating the Factory Inspectorate or setting the working day at eight hours was an inherently socialist measure. The capital of such a company is no less an exclusive possession and it remains a commodity producer. It is, however, a form of possession in which the workers have greater means of control and a further institutional basis through which to defend themselves.

NOTES

1. In an earlier article, 'Marx and Engels on Law, Crime and Morality', I stressed that although Marx regarded the state and law as media of action of the dominant class he did not, therefore, adopt the attitude that criminality is *merely* the sign of repression. This, for Marx, would be apolitical and individualistic: the criminal is a product of social relations, the *lumpenproletariat*, the criminal classes, are a political enemy, and crime, far from being a political act of class resistance, is an individual act tailor-made for repression in forms sanctioned by the bourgeois law. Criminality is an individualistic response by backward and pauperised sections of the working class, not a political response by its vanguard. Further, crime in the form of theft, far from violating bourgeois private property, goes along with it. To say with Prudhon 'property is theft' is to ignore the fact that property always takes definite legal forms (whether private, co-operative or collective) and that there are no 'natural' property relations. Prudhon is subscribing to a naive conception of natural rights theory which makes socialism a matter of distributive justice (restoring the natural order). A socialist economy will have *property* relations and therefore the possibility of theft. Only *communism* which makes questions of distribution and possession superfluous can dispense with property forms and therefore with their legal regulation. Subscribing as Marx did to the view that state and law (including socialism – the dictatorship of the proletariat) are forms of domination of a class did not involve a positive estimation of criminality.

2. The classic discussions of 'monopoly capital', Hilferding's *Finance Capital* Bukharin and Lenin, all conceive it as the final terminal phase of capitalism: as

in Lenin's phrase 'parasitic and decaying capitalism'. Two features are central in this 'highest stage': (i) the decay of capitalist property relations into forms of pure appropriation which are functionless in social production, capitalists become a parasitic *rentier* and speculative finance capitalist class; (ii) the cartels and trusts reflect the increasing concentration and socialisation of the units of production, capitalist organisation is forced to go beyond the limits of private property and competition. Bukharin in *Imperialism and World Economy* conceives this latter tendency as producing in its final phase a single hyper-repressive state capitalist super-trust. 'Monopoly capital' is a realisation of tendencies within the total social capital. At no point does the organisation of 'monopoly' capitalist enterprises receive serious theoretical consideration. Indeed, as we shall see for Hilferding (and Renner) the actual units of industrial production are anticipations of socialism.

Far from remedying this lack, subsequent Marxist discussion of the concept of 'monopoly capital' has concentrated on criticising apologetic and managerialist conceptions of the corporation, in particular denying the reality of the postulated divorce of ownership and control. While I am no partisan of this latter thesis, this form of criticism seems to me to miss the point – it ignores the possible effects of corporate organisations of capital by insisting that in the last instance all capitals are run by or are constrained to be run for individuals who derive their livelihood from profits on the capital advanced. Baran and Sweezy's *Monopoly Capital* does not break with these tendencies (its main innovations consist in radically modifying the theory of value), and although it goes some way toward recognising the distinctions of corporate organisation this leads to a conception of the corporation as a super-subject capable of manipulating its environment in the interests of its own survival.

3. Karl Renner (1870–1950) had a distinguished political career. Social Democrat Chancellor of the Austrian Republic between 1918–1920, he was imprisoned in 1934 in the authoritarian civil war against the Social Democrats. He became Chancellor of the reconstituted republic in 1945 and President from 1946 until his death in 1950.

Austro-Marxist literature is badly served by English translation: this is being remedied by a selection of texts published by Bottomore and Goode (1978). Kelsen is much better served. One of his major theoretical texts *General Theory of Law and the State* and a collection of essays *What is Justice?* are available in English.

Pashukanis (1891–1937) rose to prominence in Soviet legal circles after the publication of the first edition of the 'General Theory . . .'. He became Director of the Institute of Soviet Construction and Law, Vice-President of the Communist Academy and chief editor of the leading periodical *Soviet State and Law*. With the turn toward Stalinism he was forced to repudiate his earlier work, grudgingly in 1930 in the essay *Soviet State and Revolution in Law* (also translated in Babb, a document which reveals the shocking change in the climate of discussion since the mid-twenties) and more fully later. He participated actively in the drafting of the new Constitution and was nominated Vice-Commissar for Justice in 1936. In 1937 he disappeared and was shot.

Apart from the material in Babb (1951) Pashukanis' work is discussed by Schlesinger (1951) and more recently in a somewhat uncritical if enthusiastic

revival by Arthur (1967-7). Berman (1963) briefly discusses Pashukanis and deals extensively with the Soviet legal context. Sharlet (1974) discusses Pashukanis' work in the context of Soviet legal reform and practice. See also Appendix 2 in which Blanke *et al.*'s development of Pashukanis is discussed.
4. I have discussed Edelmann's work elsewhere, see my introduction to B. Edelman *La Droit saisi par la photographie* – translated by E. Kingdom as *Ownership of the Image* (1979).
5. I have discussed this mechanism of representation of the process to the agents and the theory of ideology in some detail in the chapters on ideology above, 2, 3 and 4.
6. 'Analysing the juridic relationship, we see perfectly distinctly that the logical content of the legal form comprises more than obligation . . . obligation always comes out as a reflection or correlate of a corresponding right. The category of right becomes logically complete only where the right comprises a bearer and an owner of rights – his rights being neither more nor less than the obligations of others made secure in his behalf' Pashukanis (p. 152).

It is not difficult to show that the idea of unconditional obedience to an external, norm establishing authority has nothing in common with the legal form . . . . Let us suppose . . . a military formation, where a host of people are subjected in their movements to a military order to which they conform: here the only active and autonomous principle is the will of the commander.

Ibid (p. 154)

7. This is what the classic historical materialist thesis – 'It is not the consciousness of man that determines their being, but, on the contrary, their social being that determines their consciousness' – amounts to. In its simplest form as the reflection theory, reality generates its own representations which are interiorised by the subject. Reality, the objective as opposed to consciousness, generates the contents of consciousness, its own representation. For a critique of this conception and also of attempts to modify it by means of the notion of 'representation', see Chapter 3.
8. The constraints and limitations imposed on political and other practices by legislative procedure and legal forms vary between the constitutional forms and legal systems of different states. Such procedures and forms suppose certain types of political practices and prohibit or limit others. The degree of constraint offered by the constitution and the legal system depends on the balance of political forces supporting their operation as semi-autonomous spheres. The degree of constraint and specific effect can vary between different spheres of legality and legal practice. It is obviously highest where the 'separation of powers' is effective in the practice of institutions, that is, where courts and rules of adjudication are relatively immune to direct pressure from within the administrative hierarchy and able to respond to wider political pressures in their own way. The obvious example is the US legal system. Kirchheimer (1961) stresses the possibilities of this differential legal autonomy in a very clear way.

The nature of legal effectivities can be exemplified by conditions in which they are threatened, in which the dominant political forces engage in practices to which certain existing legal institutions, forms and laws constitute limits. We will take the example of Nazi ideology and practice toward constitutionality and law. After the debacle of the 1923 Putsch, Hitler committed the NSDAP to a seizure of power by constitutional means and within constitutional forms. Hitler accepted the terms of legality only as conditions dictated by the necessities of political struggle. He adopted the position that bourgeois-democratic forms were an arena of struggle: 'The Constitution only maps out the arena of battle, not the goal. We enter the legal agencies and in that way will make our party the determining factor. However, once we possess the constitutional power, we will mould the state into the shape we hold to be suitable'. (Cited by Bracher, p. 245.) Before and after 1933 Hitler was careful to act within the Constitution, his Party's actions legitimated by the pen of Hindenburg. As Bracher points out this was possible because of the nature of the emergency provisions in the Weimar Constitution. Hitler's government was a constitutional one and remained broadly within the forms of law.

Nazi ideology posited a new form of state: a state expressing a particular race-community (*Volksgemeinschaft*) and organised on the Leader Principle. This ideology produced a particular theory of law. The concept of law as a sphere of rules and adjudication distinct from politics could not easily be accommodated with this conception of the state. In a world of races locked in struggle for supremacy and survival the will of the race-community expressed through its Leader must dominate and can be constrained by no formal limits. Nazi legal theorists criticised the very notion of the specificity and autonomy of the legal apparatuses from popular, Party and government control as 'Jewish-capitalist' (bourgeois liberalism), an absurd limit on *volkisch* sentiments and the Leader's will. Nazi legal theory posited rules and procedures of adjudication which were a mixture of the authoritarian and popular: popular sentiment and opinions (racial outrage, etc.) should dictate the classification of acts and the scale of punishment, rules became norms of performance dictated by the Leader and were subjected to idealisation as the standard embodied by the true member of the race-community. This conception was far from realised.

Nazi legal philosophy served as the rationale for the modification of existing institutions. The Nazis proposed to obviate the constraints offered by the forms of legislative procedure by means of the doctrine that 'the Führer's will has the force of law' – lawyers and judges, government officials should accept any statement of the Leader as having the force of statute and act accordingly. The Leader's will is supposed to be immediate, retrospective and subject only to interpretation by him (and by him through Party and state). This conception depends on the ideological/political compliance of the personnel. Given this it negates *as doctrine* every inconvenient instance of procedure and legality. In practice however, it requires the promulgation, interpretation, acceptance and practicality of rules, norms and procedures thus enunciated. To espouse the notion of immediate effectivity is not to realise it.

In respect of the constraints on political action and objectives involved in existing statute law and the process of adjudication certain Nazi theorists espoused a conception of crime and the criminal which again was supposed to take care of any inconvenient instance. The basis for the assessment of crime is the sentiments and standards of the race-community, represented by its higher types and leaders. Laws became a norm of conduct, a norm represented by the ideal racial individual and defined by Party and Leader. Limiting crime to definite classes of act and event and criminals to persons responsible for them is liberal formalism. Acts against existing statute law but which are committed on the basis of race sentiment or in the struggle to create the new order are not crimes (hence the amnesty for SA men convicted under Weimar and the dismissal of proceedings against persons abusing Jews). Lawyers and judges (as members of the race-community) are to be partisan, to act from sentiment and follow political direction. Acts not prohibited in the conventional criminal law could become offences meriting severe punishment, the nature of these acts is determined entirely by judicial discretion (the criminal is a type to be recognised by 'phenomenological' methods, not the positive determination of events). Thus 'the degeneration of racial will to work' is a crime and such a state of the individual's motivation (it was not evidenced by any particular class of acts) is a matter of pure attribution of judgement.

Nazi practice was no simple actualisation of Nazi ideology. The Nazi regime found statute law in general workable, judges and lawyers co-operative and sympathetic to the new regime. Despite a rejection in ideology of the basis of the existing legal forms and procedures Nazi political practice did not attempt to remove the existing apparatuses and completely replace them with practices based on the new principles. The People's Court paralleled but did not replace existing judicial organs. Nazi legal 'reform' was limited, being concentrated in the areas of labour law and on the introduction of a legal basis for racial discrimination against the Jews. The major innovations in the institutions of state (concentration camps, special police, institutions, etc.) had little to do with the establishing of the race-community as a reality and populstic conceptions of norms and practice. These institutions, moreover, paralleled and circumvented rather than replaced the legal apparatuses.

While lawyers and the Nazis co-existed happily, the results of conventional legal practice did little to confirm or realise Nazi legal theory. Adjudication did not follow the new procedures suggested by the ideologies, and it remained a distinct practice of legal specialistis and governed by specific rules. The new severity in criminal judgement and punishment urged after 1934 ground to a halt, overflowing prisons gave way to amnesties and the return of fines to prominence (Nazi theorists despised the fine as a calculating, plutocratic and irrational punishment, conceiving corporal punishment and humiliation as preferable because acting on the spirit) as Rusche and Kirchheimer (Ch. X and XI) demonstrate. [On Nazi conceptions of law see Kirchheimer (1940) (1961), Neumann (1942), Rusche and Kirchheimer (1939) and Stern (1975). On the Nuremburg Laws, special state institutions and the persecution of the Jews see Krausnick and Brozat (1970)]

Populantzas in *Fascism and Dictatorship* recognises that Weimar Law remained largely intact. He argues that this is primarily so in the sphere of private law, the regulation of property relations. This retention he attributes to the fact that the Weimar legal system was already a developed expression of the relations of monopoly capitalism and was therefore adequate because fascism is a specific variant of the interventionist imperialist state. Poulantzas couples this retention of private law (with its functionally necessary role in the economy) with a characterisation of the Nazi regime as an 'exceptional state form' in which the framework of public law ceases to function. He advances two theses about the legal character of the fascist state; grossly condensed here, they are as follows: '1. Law . . . no longer regulates: arbitrariness reigns . . . 2. Law is no longer the limit . . .' (Poulantzas, p. 322). Broadly he adopts the position of Neumann that in the Nazi state the rule of law and the formal structures of legality are overthrown. Neumann utilises the classic political-philosophical concept of arbitrary power or despotism, a regime whose very principle of functioning is opposed to law. This opposition (despotism/rule of law) has a long history from Bodin to Montesquieu and beyond: it involves a philosophical general concept of legality, law as an essence which can be present or absent. Poulantzas is using an opposition which has served, for example, to justify French absolutism by contrasting it with the rule of the Turk. Only if law can be displaced by being contradicted in *its principles*, if it has an essence which can be violated, can it be true to say that arbitrariness reigns without limit. If one rejects this philosophical essentialisation of law then even though legal apparatuses are subject to considerable political interdiction they are not necessarily denied all social effects, and these can become increasingly important as the regime's general nature becomes more repressive. A good example is modern South Africa where the autonomy of procedures of ajudication and the relative immunity of legal representatives have until recently provided a valuable arena for political agitation and a limited means of defence (Kirchheimer 1961 makes this point very well).

In Nazi Germany courts and prisons remained distinct institutions from the Gestapo, the SS and the camps: it depended into whose hands individuals fell, how they or their acts were classed, how they were treated. In this respect certain *concepts* of the rule of law are violated (universality of form, identity of treatment for acts of the same class, etc.) but law does not cease to exist or operate. The legal system of the *Ancien Regime*, before the principles of Beccaria and the reformers, had no such concept of necessary consistency of institutions or practice, the courts and the system of *Lettre de cachet* existed side by side, class and ecclesiastical privileges in trial and punishment prevailed, torture was an accepted means of evidence and proof. This was a legal *system*, its principles of rationalisation differed from the ones which are still current. The value of the legal conceptions of classical liberalism, of a universal and uninterrupted set of civil rights and liberties (calculable and not subject to political interdiction), is not in dispute here. My objective is merely to point out that in terms of operation and effect legal systems can exist when not in conformity with such standards. Political systems which violate these standards are not without limits to power or forms of legality.

Even if the familiar legal institutions and concepts were wholly eliminated the exercise of power would not be *arbitrary*: it would be constrained by the means of its exercise (as Poulantzas well knows) and it would have conditions and categories acting on its determination. To consider that the fascist state '. . . does not even lay down rules for functioning. It has no *system*' (Poulantzas, p. 322) is to deny that it is organised and has categories for its institutions. It is to refuse to take the Nazi conception of state seriously or to measure it by the standards of liberal constitutionality. While Nazi practice was by no means consistent with its own ideology (which had many contradictory and divergent strands), the Nazi state both retained existing institutions (and de facto their codes of practice) and created new ones (office of Four Year Plan, 'SS state' institutions, etc.), *no* state ever is a mere actualisation of constitutional principles the 'liberal democratic' state being no exception. The Nazis did, however, create practices and institutions which made the 'leader state' based on the invocation of a race-community all too much of a reality. The murder of communists and the opposition, the exclusion and extermination of the Jews, the hobbling of the Werhmacht and civil service during the war, were part of a political programme and attempts to constitute a political system. Systematic racism and the Leader Principle is, however detestable, the programme for a definite form of state.

9. Crime and punishment . . . acquire their juridic nature – on the basis of the redemption arrangement. Criminal law is thus integrated as a component part of the juridic superstructure inasfar as it embodies one of the varieties of the basic form to which modern society is subordinate: the form of equivalent exchange with all the consequences deriving therefrom. Realisation of this relationship in the criminal law is one of the aspects of realising the *Rechtstaat* as an ideal form of the intercourse of independent and equal goods-producers encountering each other in the market. But inasmuch as social relationships are not limited to the abstract relationships of abstract goods possessors, the criminal court is not merely the embodiment of an abstract form of law but also an instrumentality of direct class struggle. And the more sharp and intense the course of that struggle, the more difficult the realisation of class dominance in the form of law. In that event, the position of the 'impartial' court with its gurantees is occupied by an organisation of immediate and summary class despotism whose acts are guided solely by considerations of political expediency.

                                                              Pashukanis (p. 214)

10. Or rather, are committed in intention to retreating from some of its effects. Most of these tendencies have failed even to consider coming to terms with the fundamental Marxist concepts which are productive of those politically 'unacceptable' effects, for example, the concept of the state as 'representative' of class society. For a discussion of the problems of this concept of state and its relation to classes, particularly attempts to give it a sophisticated reformulation in the work of Althusser and Poulantzas, see *Marx's Capital and Capitalism Today*, Vol. I., Pt. 3 and Hirst (1977).

11. The Babb translation, which fails to give the modern English equivalents of Marxist concepts, has 'form of goods'.

12. This position on socialism and law resembles Bukharin's position that as the law of value will cease to operate under socialism there cannot be a socialist political economy, c.f. *Economics of the Transition Period*. In both cases the form in question is derived directly from the commodity form and the law of value.

It should be noted that Pashukanis' position that there could be no 'Proletarian' law, whilst marking him out as a left Bolshevik, did not commit him to the view that arbitrariness and authoritarianism were therefore acceptable.

13. This conception of society comes out most clearly in a text available in

English, Hilferding's critique of Bohm-Bawerk. cf. *Bohm-Bawerk's Criticism of Marx* (especially pp. 133–4).

14. Patriarchial social relationships are supposed by Renner here, the head disposes of the goods and labour of the whole household.

15. Renner identifies 'property' with the modern Roman law conception, possession of things by an individual human subject. O.Kahn-Freund in a most helpful introduction to *The Institutions* . . . points out that no such simple category of property rights exists in English law.

16. Renner's theoretical position thus happily corresponds with his reformist and legalist conception of socialisation. The government changes the property form purely by legislative action, the rest is a matter of technical economic operation. But this theoretical position is not produced by reformism, Marx too considers the enterprise as a socialised form. See Marx's *Capital and Capitalism Today* Vol. 1, Pt. 2., Ch. 5.

17. c.f. *The Modern Corporation and Private Property*.

18. See 'Humanism and Teleology in Sociological Theory', Hindess (1977) for a discussion of this concept.

19. This conception of the corporation as a constitutive subject is the dominant mode in which the specificity of the corporation as a distinct form of organisation of capital has been conceived, for example, Drucker's *The Concept of the Corporation*. The managerialist literature has its left reflection in much of the discussion of monopolies and multi-national companies which treat them as all-powerful entities capable of realising their will.

20. The concepts of possession/separation, economic agent and enterprise as unit of possession/economic subject are extensively discussed in Vol. 1, Chs, 10–12 of *Marx's Capital and Capitalism Today*.

21. A thorough discussion if the current legal position of the joint-stock company is Hadden *Company Law and Capitalism*.

22. We refer the reader to a number of excellent papers which provide the beginnings of a Marxist analysis of the British financial system and which step outside of the theoretical obstacles of classical Marxism, see Fishman (1976), Thompson (1976) (1977) and Hussain (1976).

23. See Thompson (1977).

24. Insurance companies and pension funds were major sources of finance for property speculators and subsequently entered the property boom themselves, see Marriot (1967).

25. This discussion is largely taken from Formoy (1923) and Hunt (1936).

26. Formoy, p. 47.

27. Inasmuch as transferable shares become in a measure part of the circulation of the country and as there will always be an extensive class of buyers and sellers of shares thus made publicly vendible by sanction of law, many of which buyers and sellers will be . . . inexperienced persons, it is the duty of the legislature to keep some degree of control over the birth and course of life of joint-stock companies, having reference to the different objects for which they may be formed.

Evidence, Report of 1844 – cited Hunt, p. 96.

. . . the legislature was induced to interfere in passing the Act (of 1844) not for the purpose of giving facilities to the creation and operation of those bodies; but for the protection of the public.

Bunyan, *Law of Life Insurance*, cited Hunt, p. 97

28. cited Hunt, p. 74.

29. The editor of the *Quarterly Mining Review*, July 1835, was critical of the virtues of the joint-stock promotions in mining: 'We are yet to see whether mines, although worked by private individuals, can be carried on with *equal* advantages and benefit by a company. . . . It seldom requires a company composed of £5 scrip shares to work a mine which is deserving of attention, as adequate capital may be raised by other means', cited Hunt, p. 77.

Another authority writing in 1843, having considered the eighty-one British mining companies having a paid-up capital of £4,500,000, remarked as follows: 'For the greater part they are not only complete failures, but are memorable proofs of the folly and cupidity of British capitalists on the one hand, and the knavery of their projectors on the other', cited Hunt, p. 77.

While these remarks display the conservative anti-corporate ideology they nevertheless show that joint-stock forms of organisation were far from being considered a necessity by informed contemporaries.

30. Most of these utilities were only marginally connected with industrial production, the water companies being primarily for the provision of drinking water, for example. What motivated their projectors to see incorporation was not the *size* of the capital but the prolonged period over which it would have to be amortised.

31. The primary object of limited liability being to let small and non-capitalist investors make use of their savings with minimal risk, to encourage thrift, and to protect the respectable mass of middling means not to bolster the capital market.

32. This *lassez faire* policy is commonly conceived as an *absence* of state intervention, yet it can clearly be seen to be a particular form of state intervention, a public policy pursued by means of legislation.

33. Marx *does*, however, cite the reports on the Bank Acts.

34. An excellent example of the consequences of mergers engineered by companies seeking quick profits through 'rationalisation', written by a manager, is Hope's 'On being taken over by Slater-Walker'.

35. For a discussion of company organisation in Japan see Bieda, *The Structure and Operations of the Japanese Economy*, and Patrick and Rosovsky (eds), *Asia's New Giant*, Ch. 7.

36. More explicit provisions about the right to dividend and its level would have to be introduced in that case. Hadden (1972, 2nd edition 1977) discusses various prospects of reform of company law and the legal position of worker's co-operatives.

Appendix 1. Pashukanis and the Legal Subject

Pashukanis argues that the 'subject is the atom of juridic theory' and that 'every sort of juridic relationship is a relationship between subjects' (p. 160). Yet the *legal* subject, its attributes and constitution receive no attention in Pashukanis' text. The specific form of the legal subject is unproblematic. Pashukanis resolves the legal subject into the economic subject, just as he resolves the legal form into the commodity form. The legal subject is considered as the possessive bearer of right, an abstraction from the concrete possessor of labour products/commodities. Possessive right therefore appears to be derived from the actual relations of possession in commodity society. Right is explicable by the prior relationship of the economic subject to things.

Pashukanis is right to give the category of subject a central place in his conception of law. Law is essentially the interaction of subjects, and subjects whose attributes are socially given to the legal sphere. Defining private law as a sphere in which subjects enter into contest over rights (essentially rights of possession) is plausible on two conditions:

(i) that, as we have seen, the role of public law in defining this sphere and of the state in furnishing its apparatuses is either ignored or denied any significance;

(ii) *that right and possession can be equated*, right is merely the recognition of existing forms of possession and the essential content of rights is possession.

Pashukanis can thus ignore the legal subject and rights as *specific legal constructs*, operative within and dependent on definite and specific legal apparatuses. Law is merely another form of 'expression' of the economic subject and its relation to things.

Let us now question in detail Pashukanis' definition of the legal sphere.

1   LAW IS A REALM OF EQUIVALENT SUBJECTS IN CONTEST

It is correct that the subjects confronting one another in, say, modern British civil law are formally *equal* – all have an equal right to act as subjects in the law, to initiate suits, etc, and are equal before the law, that is, status is not deemed to prejudice judgement. But they are not *identical* in legal definition and status. Thus, excluding minors, we have public bodies, corporations, companies, partnerships, trusts and 'private' individuals. The obligations and responsibilities placed on these distinct legal statuses and the rights accorded to them differ considerably; for example, individuals are not as such subject to the provisions and requirements of the Companies Acts, to file accounts, to hold annual meetings, etc. These differences in status overlap with and contribute to the differentiation in the types of legal disputes and actions: for example, a trust cannot get married and therefore cannot petition for divorce or sue for custody of children. Subjects in law and the relations of dispute between them are not homogeneous. Pashukanis, in order to treat the legal form as an outgrowth of the commodity form, must erase these differences or reduce them to analogues of the relation between the person and the thing in his conception of commodity relations. Thus he must treat differences in the legal status of subjects as 'fictions', corporate bodies being reducible to human individuals, or as secondary elaborations of conditions in which legal and economic subjects coincide in the person of the commodity-bearer.

2 POSSESSION IS THE FOUNDATION OF RIGHT

Economic possession for Pashukanis is the real foundation of property right and, therefore, of the category of right in general. Commodity relations are conceived as producing a single general possession-form (relation between persons and things) and one which can be identified as independent of and determinative of its legal expression. *But relations of possession cannot be specified in general.* Firstly, forms of possession can only be specified in terms of particular economic conditions and production processes: only in this way is it possible to determine who or what has a particular form of effective disposition over the elements entering into the production process and over its products (this argument is developed in detail in Hindess and Hirst 1977). Forms of 'possession' are not equivalent, even within relations of commodity exchange, they cannot in consequence serve as the origin of an homogeneous category of right as Pashukanis wants possession to do. Secondly, commodity relations are capable of existing in conjunction with many different forms of possession (that is, effective disposition: examples of such diverse forms of possession operating through sales and purchases are merchants' capital operating a 'putting-out' system and modern industrial workers' co-operatives). Moreover, markets do not entail similar conditions of sale and purchase. Thus there are different market forms for different types of commodities, not all of which correspond to the notions of 'alienable things', or 'products of labour' involved in the theory of fetishism. Life assurance, company shares, commodity 'futures' in no sense correspond to 'products of labour' or material 'use-values', such commodities consist in promises as to future acts and depend on being defined in legal forms which make those promises obligations. *Possession here depends upon and consists in rights*, shares or insurance policies are *titles* to income on certain conditions. Public-organised markets like grain exchanges depend upon specific legal rules to make certain forms of sale and purchase possible, in other legal contexts these forms have been expressly forbidden as, for example, speculating on the harvest. Possession and commodity relations in large part take their form from and are differentiated by legal institutions, rules and rights. Possession and exchange have both economic *and* legal conditions of existence, the legal form cannot be treated as a derivation.

3   RIGHT IS ANALOGOUS TO POSSESSION

Pashukanis conceives the essence of law as 'possessive right'. The relation of the subject to the right is a *proprietal* one (it is 'his' right to something) and the content of the right is a *possession*, an alienable thing. This unduly restricts the category of rights. Rights are legally defined and sanctioned capacities to act in certain ways and to enjoy certain conditions. Political rights, freedom of assembly, security of correspondence, etc., are not possessions but circumstances defined in and granted by statute. Pashukanis dismisses them as an ideological gloss on class dictatorship and as formed by analogy with private right. But rights in private law are not confined to the proprietal-possession form. Not all acts and conditions in private law relate to possession and exchange: marriage and divorce, minority and wardship, libel, etc., concern the statuses and capacities of subjects. Questions of property do not exhaust or even dominate the legal definition of marriage, childhood, etc. It would be absurd to treat divorce suits as merely the regulation of married persons' property or libel actions as being merely concerned with economic standing. Property and possession cannot explain the differentiated gamut of legal rights. The whole range of rights in private law cannot be treated as derivatives of possession.

4   LAW IS A RELATION BETWEEN SUBJECTS

Pashukanis' conception of the law as subjects in contest pursuing rights treats law much like the conventional conception of a market, that is, as the interaction between the subjects entering into exchange. But neither law nor markets can be treated as inter-subjective relations. With an organised market like a stock exchange or money market this can easily be seen to be not the case, public policy, legal regulation and market institutions define the nature of the commodity, who is permitted to trade and the practices relating to sales and purchases. *All* developed commodity relations have in some measure the character of organised markets (thus things like trade credit or hire purchase, essential to a large proportion of sales, are economic institutions with conditions of existence outside those of the two parties to the sale such as government credit control policies, the operations of finance houses, etc.). Pashukanis ignores in his definition of the legal form not only legislation, as we have seen, but also the courts as institutions, the position of the judge, the role of legal interpretation, etc. In his conception these must be at best secondary to and derived effects of the relation of subjects one to another. How the subjects can enter into *legal* relations except through the effects of these apparatuses and practices is obscure. Law is left without a definite organisational form and that form without specific effects in Pashukanis' conception. We have seen that this must be so if legal forms are to have a prior social origin in what is conceived as private and unplanned (commodity) relations between subjects. This 'materialist' analysis ignores the institutions and practices of the law.

PASHUKANIS AND LOCKE

Pashukanis conceives the essence of law as 'possessive right'. As we have seen, law is constructed by derivation from the social relations of simple commodity production. The proprietal relationship of the individual subject to things reflects the fact that men are separated from one another as independent private producers. Labour (appropriation of nature) in a privatised form creates individual possession. Men enter into relations with one another as the bearers of their labour products and in order to exchange those products. Exchange, in *transferring* things, mediates between different concrete labours and reproduces both parties as a possessor. Equivalence is necessary to exchange in order to reproduce the conditions (possession) of privatised production. The recognition of possessive right in the form of law is thus an expression of both the *socialness* of exchange and the *privatisation* of production.

Pashukanis' construction of law by derivation from a concept of social relations has certain resemblances to another, John Locke's analysis of property right in *The Second Treatise of Government*. Locke, in order to explain the laws of civil society, presupposes a non-political condition of human life which he calls the 'state of nature'. Men are independent of one another ('men' here represents the households of patriarchs, including women and servants), without formal association or government. Locke derives government from a 'compact' of the independent subjects. But this 'government' is a mere *socialisation* of an existing condition, in the state of nature each man is a magistrate of the 'law of nature' and judge in his own cause. 'Civil government' arises from the difficulties of this enforcement. Law does not arise in the compact but, as the law of nature, is given by God. The state of nature is governed by its law and this law is apprehended by men by means of their 'natural reason'. All men are created by God and are His property; *as such* (as His) they are forbidden to injure one another, since to do so is to violate God's right of possession. Law, apparently founded on God's Will, is based on property right (God is conceived as Locke conceives the proprietal subject). Locke's theory of (earthly) property is that God has granted the use of the earth and its fruits to man. Men are *possessors of themselves*: 'Though the Earth, and all inferior Creatures be common to all Men, yet every Man has a Property in his own Person. This no Body has any Right to but himself' (*2nd. Treatise*, p. 328). Possessors of themselves, men also have the right to their own *attributes*. To alienate an attribute is clearly to alienate oneself (and hence to violate the possession of self), since attributes are inseparable from the subject and definitive of it. Labour is an attribute of man, hence men have a right to their labour by reason of their possession of themselves. Labour is appropriation of nature. It follows that, labour being inseparable from its products, men have a right to the *products* of their labour.

Mens' association in civil government is possible because they have a right to preserve themselves and their property, and are constrained by natural law not to violate others' rights. These rights and obligations arise from the fact that they each are God's property. Property law is founded on the originary possession by the subject of itself. God is the First Subject. God constrains men to act in certain ways because they are the fruits of *His labour* and thus His property. Property law thus, far from being grounded on God's Will, grounds and justifies that Will. *God is conceived as a subject of possessive right*. That subject is prior-possessive to itself, to its own attributes.

In both Pashukanis and Locke the proprietal subject is the central category. For Pashukanis the subject is possessor *because his labours take a determinate social form*. For Locke products of labour are property by reason of the constitutively proprietal nature of the subject. Pashukanis grounds the law on the necessity of its social function: on ensuring the forms of possession necessary to the reproduction of the agents of production, it thus arises to secure a prior and real relation of possession. Locke grounds civil law on the will of human subjects ('compact') and the natural law, which makes such human interaction possible, on the Will of God (men are the products of God's labour, created as *possessors* in His image). It cannot be argued that Pashukanis' position is analogous to Locke's in the theoretical means by which it is constructed. However, both of them conceive property rights (on the basis of their differing means) as *proprietal* in nature, the recognition of a real possession by a subject, and both conceive civil law as the recognition of a prior state of affairs. For both the subjects of possession are given prior to the process of legal recognition. There is thus a real similarity in the priority of the subject to law and the proprietal conception of right and law, that rights are possessions of the subject. This leads both derivations of the law (by different means) into a common impasse, as we shall see.

In Pashukanis' discourse the priority of the subject arises from and is made possible by the *ontological* primacy of labour;

materialism means that the subjects constitute themselves and their 'possessions' in producing their means of subsistence. Locke's subject is an instance of a different kind of priority. The explanation offered in the *Second Treatise* utilises a discursive device, the positing of a prior subject or realm of subjects and the derivation from this of the category to be explained (in this case law), which is not confined to juridico-political discourse. This same device can be found in explanations of the origin of languages and in accounts of the genesis of knowledge from sensation. It is a central element in a range of philosophical discourses, by no means confined to 'contract theory' or to one particular school of philosophy.

In the seventeenth and eighteenth centuries rights are widely conceived on the analogy with property. In the natural rights doctrines of this period rights are commonly conceived as attributes of the subject by means of the model of possessions, as appropriate to the subject by reason of a claim or right it can advance. Even if, as in Locke's argument or in the assertions of the American Declaration of Independence, rights are given by God (the Declaration uses the proprietal metaphor of an *endowment*), God is either thought of as Himself a subject with attributes, or is a passive anchorage for a subject which pursues its affairs and rights without Divine direction or hindrance. The relation of the subject to its attributes is thought through a particular philosophical concept of subject. The subject is a locus prior to and appropriative of its attributes.

This concept of subject as an *epistemological-ontological point* is given its classic formulation by Descartes in the *Discourse on Method*. The subject is the prior (already presupposed) point of inspection-possession, identifying (and therefore annexing) experiences and attributes as its own. Possession stems from *identification* ('I think therefore I am'): the subject is *possessor of itself*, capable of constituting itself in the moment of identifying thoughts as *its own* (proper-proprietal to it). The subject is a pure epistemological-ontological point, a pure (without attributes) entity of inspection which establishes the attributes proper to it by *identifying* them. It is a point which establishes its nature by recognising itself as object to itself, as an outside which it claims as its own. Locke in the *Essay on Human Understanding* adopts this Cartesian concept of subject even though he rejects Descartes' dualism. The subject as epistemological point is necessary to classical empiricism. Thus this concept is necessarily retained even in an epistemology with pretensions to thoroughgoing sensationalism like Condillac's. The point is necessary to establish the identity of experiences, without this locus of identification/recognition then sensations and their effects as experience must be fragmented and dispersed. The subject's coherence and discursive priority explains how it is possible for sense experiences to cumulate, it makes possible general categories of knowledge on the basis of sensation (it thus makes classical empiricist epistemology possible: Hacking (1975) gives an interesting discussion of this).

This concept of subject also makes possible a proprietal theory of right. (Macpherson (1962) recognises certain of the effects in political theory of what he calls 'possessive individualism'. He attributes this discursive construction to the direct effect of social relations in theory, the nascent outlook of capitalistic private property. But he does not investigate the *concepts* of subject and possession involved, identifying them with categories operative in social relations. But Locke's concept of subject is a discursive device, a point constructed in a certain mechanism of writing in order to derive categories operative in social relations.) Rights like experiences can be considered as attributes of the subject-point, defining the subject and yet possessed (appropriated in recognition) by the prior point which is distinct from them. It is this concept of subject which makes the seventeenth and eighteenth century critical concept of *natural right* other than absurd: rights which are essential attributes of the subject and yet which are not simply constitutive of it as a nature, the subject can be thought alongside and separate from its rights. If rights are *natural* it might appear that they are inalienable in a radical sense, to violate these rights is to violate the nature and therefore the existence of the subject. This device avoids natural rights' degeneration into an ontology, right and the being it defines being coincident. *Inalienable* rights are the property of the subject, rights which are his in the same way that a patrimony is. Thus rights can be held to *belong* to the subject, to be attributes appropriate to the subject's nature, even though it is concretely denied them. The subject can be thought in distinction from its attributes, and in identification of them is capable of constituting itself. The priority of the subject in critical discourses on rights makes possible the establishment of the natural and the protest of its violation. Inalienable rights which are violated would otherwise be an absurdity. Right is a property of the subject, recognised by it and claimed for it in critical discourse.

This concept of subject cannot be other than prior-proprietal to everything which it confronts. It claims itself for what it is, it annexes its nature in recognition of its own. The problem with this conception of possessive right is located precisely in this mechanism. The attributes of the subject are constituted by its (proprietal) identification, but the subject which identifies and claims is prior and *without properties*. I have called it an epistemological-ontological point because, like its geometric analogue, it is an abstraction necessary to a certain form of discourse and proof. Just as a geometric point is a spatial location without extension, so the subject is a point of recognition (an existence) without attributes. Right is annexed by the subject in possession, established as appropriate to the subject by its claim. But it is not thereby explained as right rather than some other attribute. What differentiates the sphere of rights from other attributes annexed in recognition, thoughts, senations, etc.? How does the theory of possessive right determine the specifically legal form of the right? Possession merely establishes a relation between the right and the subject. The primacy of the subject, its identification, guarantees this relation but not what is involved in the relation. The ontology of the self-possessive subject ensures the *emptiness* of the point (expelling theories of a given nature in which the subject cannot stand in opposition to its attributes because they constitute it). It also ensures the inexplicability of the attributes it annexes except in terms of its own recognition. It *claims* the right, this neither explains right as such nor the basis of the subjects' claim. The prior possessive-subject is a discursive mechanism for grounding and justifying what exists in the form of its claims.

Rights are not explained by being possessed by a subject any more than they are explained by derivation from commodities (possessions in circulation). The legal subject, as we have tried to show above and in *Marx's Capital and Capitalism Today*, cannot be explained prior to and independent of the process of legal definition. To do so is to identify rights and non-rights, to obliterate the specificity of *legal* effects. In this case, as with Pashukanis, the whole range of statuses and capacities given to subjects within the legal sphere are reduced to analogues of possessions and are conceived as attributes of a prior (extra-legal) subject. This priority of the subject, whether in Locke or Pashukanis, supposes the identity-reducibility of legally defined subjects to some category of subject prior to and outside of legal definition. Laws as a specific object of analysis disappear.

Appendix 2. Pashukanis in Modern Theory

Pashukanis' work has been an important influence on a number of recent German writers on the theory of the state. The most systematic use of the *General Theory of Law and Marxism* in this respect appears to be Blanke, Jürgens and Kastendiek's 'On the Current Marxist Discussion on the Analysis of the Form and Function of the Bourgeois State' (1974, translated in Holloway and Picciotto, 1977). These three authors are contributing to a body of work which attempts to 'derive' the form of the state in capitalism from the necessities of capitalist production relations.

This German discussion starts from the problem of why the *state*, a specific form separated from economic relations, is necessary to capitalism. Blanke *et al.* attempt to explain the conditions for the separation of the public and private spheres created by commodity/capitalist relations, and to explain why this separation makes necessary a 'state' based on the rule of law and embodying public coercive force. They begin by criticising a number of other approaches:

(i) Like other contributors to this discussion they pose the problem that treating the state as an instrument of coercion serving the interests of the capitalist class does not answer the question why this coercion takes this form? Pashukanis posed a similar question when trying to defend the specificity of the form of law, that law is not merely another example of class coercion, and the contributors to this discussion attempt to extend this question to the state in general:

Why does the dominance of a class not continue to be that which it is – that is to say, the subordination of one part of the population to another part? Why does it take the form of official state domination? Or, which is the same thing, why is not the mechanism of state constraint created as the private mechanism of the dominating class? Why is it dissociated from the dominant class – taking the form of an impersonal mechanism of public authority isolated from society?

Pashukanis (p. 185)

(ii) Unlike several other contributors to this discussion they argue that the 'derivation' of the state from the logic of capitalist relations is a limited exercise in theoretical abstraction. The specificity and limits of this theoretical operation must be recognised if two errors are to be avoided. The first error is to start with a 'general concept' of the state which is to be derived. The second error is to attempt to derive the state as a concrete instance in modern bourgeois society with all its attached apparatuses and social functions. In both case the effect of the supposed 'derivation' will be merely to reproduce the given forms as they appear, ascribing them to the necessities of the capitalist mode of production. Blanke *et al.* separate what they call 'form analysis' and 'historical analysis': form analysis attempts to demonstrate the necessity and possibility of a separate public legal-coercive instance but does not pretend to determine the state in its concrete form of existence. The analysis makes possible 'the conceptual reconstruction of the empirical, historical concrete state in specific bourgeois societies' (Blanke *et al.*, p. 114) by providing theoretical means which guide 'historical analysis' of the specific determinations. They insist that it is necessary to start from the most basic commodity-capitalist relations and not from some positive concept of the state:

We believe the state can be analysed systematically only when every pre-conceived concept of state has been abandoned, when mere associations and immediately, empirically derived notions of 'state' (whether authoritarian or parliamentary-democratic) do not infiltrate the initial stages of the enquiry as premises. The 'state' must to some extent be liberated for a theoretical reconstruction.

Blanke et al. (p. 118)

(iii) The dominant 'general concept' which leads analysis astray is that of the state-civil society separation as being between the particular private interests of individual members of the bourgeoisie and the general interests of bourgeois society. Marx in his early critiques of Hegel's concept of state retains this particular notion of the separation. The consequences of using this notion are that it is thereby supposed that the state *exists* to transcend the conditions of individual private property, its economic and social functions can thus be derived from its general concept (thus the interventionist and welfare state can be seen as a mere realisation of this defence of the general needs of bourgeois production). This makes the state appear as the rational representative of bourgeois society. Further, in this notion the class-coercive character of the state needs to be *added* to it, summed-up as merely another general interest of the bourgeoisie thus served.

Blanke *et al.* thus attempt their derivation by ignoring existing Marxist conceptions of the state. The basis for their derivation is Marx's concept of 'form' and in particular the concept of 'commodity form'. 'Form' is defined as follows:

The concept 'form' expresses both the basic problem and essential characteristic of the historical materialist method: the investigation of the connection between the material process of reproduction and the reproduction of the life of socialised people and the relations between these people who constitute themselves in this process of material reproduction.

Blanke et al. (p. 118)

The state, a separate instance, must arise as a direct necessity of and connection essential to the process of material reproduction and the social relations between men in which it is conducted. It is not definite conscious *acts* of the state with the end of promoting capitalist reproduction (intervening in crises, etc.) which are at issue, rather it is the state *as instance* which is necessary as a form to capitalist material-social reproduction. To establish the state 'we must work out from the determination of capital in general those conditions which make the genesis of a certain form *necessary*' (p. 119 – my emphasis).

The commodity form is Marx's point of departure in *Capital* in the construction of the concept of capitalist mode of production. Blanke *et al.* follow him in treating the 'society' of the commodity form, simple commodity production, as an abstraction, a necessary stage in the process of constructing the concept of CMP. Commodity relations create a society of independent private producers linked through exchange. The law of value requires a 'subjective side' (p. 121) which secures the possibility of *inter-subjective* connections between the independent agents. For the law of value to operate socially it needs to be coupled with the form of law.

Law is an essential subjective condition of exchange making possible the exchanges of matter which ensure social reproduction and which are governed by necessary objective proportionalities (law of value). Law is thus essential to the social relations between men which form the conditions for material reproduction.

Blanke *et al.* closely and explicitly follow Pashukanis in their derivation of law as form. However, in their subsequent argument they go far beyond him. They say: 'That the fundamental function of the state as a 'concrete structure' is *hidden in the form of the commodity* has so far occurred only to Marxist theoreticians specialising in law. But evidently a pre-determined concept of state has prevented them from pursuing this further' (p. 122 – my emphasis). Pashukanis, as I have shown, derives *law* from the commodity form but *not* the state. He separates law as a form regulating the relations of commodity producers and owners from the state, an instrument of class coercion. Pashukanis retains the classic Marxist-Leninist concept of state: he considers the public law form of the state as secondary and a mask for oppression, the criminal law as merely a cover for class coercion, and he cannot conceive of the institutions or means of enforcement of law (law remains a form without institutional location). His modern German followers make the *legal form* of the state a necessity for its social function. They derive the need for extra-economic coercion from the requirement that the law be enforced. From this derivation two positions follow:

(i) that the state as 'form' is defined by its function as instance and sanction of law, the state is the institutional representative of law;

(ii) the instance securing the law is defined in the form of law, and must act within that form as a specific legally-constituted and limited instance.

The sole form of state Pashukanis could derive from his form of law is the *Rechtstaat*, for him to have claimed this as the general form of state would have guaranteed his being greeted with derision in the Soviet Union. Blanke *et al.*'s position has the advantage over Pashukanis that it systematically connects public and private law, it makes the former arise as a condition of representation and enforcement of the latter.

Blanke *et al.* argue that this derivation from the commodity form in general is not problematised by the introduction of capitalist relations based on the exploitation of wage labour: '. . . the abstract categories of commodity production and circulation do not disappear with the emergence of capital as the fundamental social relation; rather they form the general categories of surface appearance' (p. 125). Law remains necessary to commodity circulation, capitalism remains a society of independent private agents even if its economic laws are based on the exploitation of labour outside of the process of exchange. Class relations are handled within the legal coercive forms appropriate to circulation, the state thus relates to the class struggle through the forms of fetishism. Capitalist class society does not change the commodity form of state and the supposition of the equality of economic agents as parties to exchange:

> This is important in understanding the fact that the formality of law and of the state based on the rule of law (*Rechtstaat*) is a functional requirement of capitalism that does not simply disappear when class structures develop.
>
> (p. 125)

The state and law, like the commodity form, are fetish forms necessary because capitalist society manifests itself as a society of exchange. The subjective conditions of the law of value remain necessary to the social process. As with Pashukanis law is essentialised as a necessary derivative of the law of value. It is assigned a particular and necessary nature, a nature set by its social origin. *The essential element in law is the regulation of property and commodity exchange.* This approach follows the others we have considered above in conceiving of capitalism as a totality which secures its conditions of existence. Fetishism is part of the logic of commodity-capitalist relations, law and the are state necessary elements in the series of fetish forms which secure its 'subjective side'. *Capital* is treated as the appropriation in concepts of a system with a logic, logical derivations from *Capital* are therefore an appropriate means of deriving positions about capitalist social relations. Logical necessity and necessity (causality) in social relations go hand in hand. This approach goes beyond the others in its consequences for the concept of state. The problem is that the concept of coercive instance of law leads to the state being derived and defined in its public law form, as representative of the law appropriate to commodity circulation, and nothing else. The remainder of the state's apparatuses and practices lie outside of 'form analysis' in the realm of particular historical products of the class struggle.

The criticisms levelled against Pashukanis' derivation of the form of law are pertinent in this case too.

1. Law is assigned an essential nature and an origin for that essence in social necessity. As we have seen this means that the

actual process of legislation and legal definition becomes at best merely the particular form in which that necessity is realised. Legislation cannot effect the content of legality. Law is a concrete generality which can be apprehended in a general concept.

Blanke *et al.* add a further twist to this by systematically linking public and private law. The state in its form as public law is not mere ideology but a fetish form which is an essential articulation of capitalist social relations. The public law form of the state is given and is necessarily commodity-capitalist, recognising the formal equality of the subjects of exchange. Political rights, equality in formal political participation (the 'worker-citizen') arise from concrete class struggles (from the material inequality of capitalism and its effects). The commodity form of state is doubled by its form as a state corresponding to political right:

> The basic form of politics too, the struggle for law and for the instance or agency guaranteeing it, the extra-economic force of coercion, is on the basis of class relations no mere illusion but the very form in which the class struggle continuing within the bourgeois state finds political expression.
>
> (p. 125)

The *Rechtstaat* is a condition for the class struggle within the forms appropriate to commodity-capitalist relations. The effect of this position is to make legislation necessarily reformist. The state is essentialised and so are practices within it. All legislation within the form of the *Rechtstaat* can only be possible if it does not exceed bourgeois limits; correspondence to public law (a condition for legislation) is correspondence to the conditions of commodity-capitalist society. Demands which cannot be so conceded and enacted are revolutionary. Blanke *et al.* argue that political rights in the *Rechtstaat* permit 'the right to aim beyond the system of the bourgeois mode of production' (p. 129). This aim cannot be realised, however, except by revolution. All demands which can be met within the form of law further institutionalise and limit the class struggle. The use of law as a means of transformation or modification of capitalist social relations is denied, the reason for this is that the form of law and its effects are essentialised (it can only be what it necessarily is).

2. Laws which are not part of the essential elements defining law, property law and contract, are considered as secondary or derivative or ignored. The core of law is 'the *proceedures* necessary to ensure the operation of the law of value' (p. 127). Law is effective at the level of circulation. The nature of law and the separation of the public and private spheres means that *within production* capital is free of legal regulation. Blanke *et al.* enthusiastically subscribe to the thesis of the despotism of capital.

Law regulates and defends *property*: 'The formal character of law applies in effect, not to its subjects but to things. Accordingly someone who possesses property is protected not as a person but as the owner of commodities, etc.' (p. 128). The legal subject exists as property owner in the sphere of circulation: 'Figuratively, the worker as *legal subject* remains forever in circulation, never entering the factory' (p. 126). This is because:

> In terms of production, the law of private property applies to the right to conform to the objective movement of the law of value in the private production process . . . and this not merely formally but through the flexible, free conduct of affairs. Here labour power counts no longer as the fine free legal subject but rather as a factor of production which the property owner can do as he wishes. . . .'
>
> (p. 128)

Blanke *et al.* have started by defining property law as primary. For them law applies to *things* and defines persons as subjects by their rights of disposition over things. But labour (or labour power) is not the capitalist's property, the worker offers definite services under a contract of employment (and these can vary widely). Blanke *et al.* tend to conflate the laws of property and contract, considering labour power as a *thing* over which the capitalist has unrestricted rights for the period of hire (to 'do as he wishes'). But contract is a relation *between persons*, what is or can be agreed can be limited by the terms of the agreement and law.

Karl Renner recognised that the law of property alone could not regulate capitalist production, for him the law of contract became increasingly important as a form of regulation of the economy. The terms of contracts are not given but there is no necessity for them to permit the employer to 'do as he wishes' or to treat the worker as he would a thing. Further, laws regulating hours of work, health and safety at work, the protection of the public, etc. limit what can be agreed and supervise the production process. To suppose that the worker is not a legal subject when at work is absurd: if injured at work he or she can sue, if called to testify against the firm in a matter involving state regulation he or she is competant as a witness, these are but two examples. The thesis of the despotism of capital supposes a particular conception of the rights of property as essential to law in capitalism and other legal conditions as derivaties of class struggle against capital. This is entirely a product of the mode of analysis chosen – property has no rights *per se*. All laws which recognise the worker as a responsible legal subject when at work can by no means be even plausibly be argued to arise from the class struggle: to take one example, the Official Secrets Acts do not allow the owners of armaments firms and other Government contractors the freedom to 'do as they wish' and likewise bind and supervise employees. A host of varied legislation, much of it of little direct benefit to workers, treats the worker at work as a legal subject and regulates his conduct.

Despotism is conceived as a necessary effect of capitalist social relations and law as representing that necessity to the agents. 'Form analysis' does not merely consider possibilities but constructs (by logical derivation from *Capital*) relations with necessary conditions of existence and necessary effects. The separation of form and history is in what it contains largely a convention imposed by the authors, whatever is not ascribed to form (to the necessary logic of the system) can be ascribed to the class struggle. This separation promotes certain categories to primacy, in this case property law, and these categories are not merely formal, definite consequences follow from them like the despotism of capital. Whatever lies outside this is ascribed to history and the class struggle. But history and the class struggle are for the authors nothing more than the concrete existence of the system and are ultimately governed by its laws of motion. In this way the postulated essence of law can be defended against apparent exceptions, as products of the workers' struggle, and that struggle itself explained as a product of the system. The result is to ascribe necessary limits to law, to capitalism and the workers' struggle. Radical changes in workers' rights, in property forms, and in economic units (say, workers' co-operatives) will be written off as reformist and contradictory to the logic of capital. Any struggles toward such objectives will be dismissed as institutionalised rather than revolutionary class struggle.

Further problems arise with the authors' position in addition to those which are analagous to Pashukanis. These are as follows.

1. The state is conceived as a definite public law form (*Rechstaat*), a form which corresponds to the conditions required by the laws essential to commodity-capitalist society and to the containment of the class struggle. Public law thus becomes an account of the state in its necessary form as an instance in capitalism. The 'surface' is the essential element in fetish forms. The forms in which states represent themselves (constitutions, etc.), or, rather are represented in rather old-fashioned textbooks of liberal political theory, are an adequate expression of their form as necessary to capitalist relations. Clearly, this poses Blanke *et al.* with a problem since the apparatuses and actions of modern capitalist states go well beyond their construction. This is solved, as before, by making additional functions and effects depend upon the class struggle and the concrete conditions of particular capitalisms. The effectivity, unity and logic of these additional functions lies *outside* of the state as formal-legal entity. It is in the '*movement of capital*' (p. 138) that the source and fate of the various policies and agencies that are attached to this 'formal unity' are to be found. Again the convenient separation of form analysis and historical analysis shows its effects here: history is made by the 'movement of capital', the laws of motion of capitalism and the class struggle resulting from them concretised in a definite historical situation.

The effect of this position is to reduce the state as separate instance proper to a minimal form, law plus enforcement plus formal political rights. Its executive, administrative and organisational capacities and effects disappear. The state is both essentialised, given a 'general concept contrary to their claims, and reduced to a combination of the nightwatchman and parliamentary-democratic states. Outside of this form is the causal primacy of the logic of capital and the class struggle incited by its effects. The states' effectivity is an illusion, the state as entrepeneur or as agency of welfare answers to the 'movement of capital'. Whilst this approach correctly challenges the conception of the state as the rational reflection of the collective interests of the bourgeoisie or as an all-powerful means of resolving the contradictions of capitalism, insisting on its limits, it essentialises these limits. The state is limited by the logic of capitalism as social totality, and not by the determinate means of exercise of its powers and the specific conditions in which it acts. The state is limited by the system which necessitates its existence and its role, its effects are determined outside of it by the general necessities of commodity-capitalist relations and by 'the movement of capital'. The capitalist mode of production is here conceived as an entity with a necessary structure and laws of motion, both are traceable to its fundamental economic law, the law of value. This totality is complicated by the insistence that these laws are realised in definite historical conjunctures, but, as we have seen, these conjunctures are ultimately the product of the system, its contradictions, and the class struggle engendered by them. It is against type of concept of totality that *Marx's Capital and Capitalism Today* was written. It renders the analysis of definite political, legal and economic relations impossible except as elements of this totality, subject to its limits of effect. We have seen how those limits constrain analysis of legal and economic forms.

2. Blanke *et al.* are driven into considering their concept of state-form in capitalism as the core of existing capitalist states. In effect the form is the 'general concept', the essential element in the state. The result of this is to make their conception of state-

form as *Rechtstaat* the *normal* form of capitalist state. They are in consequence forced to treat the Nazi regime both as an exceptional form of state (because it violates their concept of state as legal form) and as an historical anomaly, a deviation from the main line of bourgeois development. The Nazi regime is thus conceived as violating the nature of law and state in capitalism (autonomy of the private sphere, state intervention in the forms of law, parliamentary-democratic institutionalisation of the class struggle). As I have tried to show (note 8, page 146) this notion of violation betokens an essentialist concept of law. Blanke *et al.* are not concerned with law as legal principle (as philosophers of law are) but with law as having a necessary form because ancillary to the law of value. In their account the anomalous nature of the Nazi regime is resolved by certain of the formal-legal necessities of capitalism re-assessing themselves through the new institutions: thus labour reappears as a commodity in the black market, the functions of trades unions are partially re-activated in the Labour Front, etc. The Nazi regime is 'dysfunctional for capital' (p. 146), although this dysfunctionality in regimes of this type can be masked for some time by exporting its costs for reproduction through war and the plundering of labour reserves. Bourgeois states therefore have a tendency to revert to forms which are functional for capital. In challenging this I am *not* trying to assert that the Nazi regime was 'functional' for the German capitalist economy, but to challenge the very notion of functional or dysfunctional forms of state itself. This notion is possible only on the basis of a conception of a neccesary logic of capital which requires certain political-legal forms of representation. These forms are normal because the capitalist mode of production both requires them and enforces them. This type of theory has little room for states and regimes which do not correspond to its archetype of capitalist state or which are not products of socialist class struggle against capitalism. These states probably form the majority of the world's regimes. As a theory of state and law for purposes of political analysis this concept produced by the operation of 'derivation' is quite useless.

Blanke *et al.* consider the capitalist state as a 'form', a necessary but fetishised representative of capitalist relations. It is necessarily a phenomenon of the 'surface' of capitalist society, securing the relations of circulation and making them the content of its forms. The separation of state and civil society, the legal form of state, are thus fetish forms, necessary to the subjective articulation of capitalist relations but occluding its inner objective determinations. The state's autonomy is thus one of the illusions necessary to the process. The state is explained as a separate instance but only paradoxically by a radical reduction of its composition and capacities. Its very *separation* becomes a fetish form governed by the totality which constitutes it as such. The state is thus essentialised, capitalist states have a basic nature as form, and are systematically determined by the logic of the mode of production and 'the movement of capital'. As in Pashukanis, but by different means, the state and the conditions of its action are grossly reduced and simplified. Those looking for an account of modern state relations in their complexity and specificity should look elsewhere.

References

Althusser, Louis, 'Marxism and Humanism', in *For Marx* (Allen Lane, London, 1969).

Althusser, Louis, 'Ideology and Ideological State Apparatuses' and 'Freud and Lacan', in *Lenin and Philosophy and Other Essays* (New Left Books, London, 1971).

Althusser, Louis and Balibar, Etienne, *Reading Capital* (New Left Books, London, 1970).

Arthur, Chris, 'Towards a Materialist Theory of Law', *Critique*, 7 (Winter, 1976–7).

Babb, Hugh W., *Soviet Legal Philosophy* (Harvard University Press, Cambridge, Mass., 1951).

Baran, Paul R. and Sweezy Paul M., *Monopoly Capital* (Penguin Books, Harmondsworth, 1968).

Beida, K., *The Structure and Operation of the Japanese Economy* (Wiley, Sydney, 1970).

Berle Adolf A. and Means, Gardiner C., *The Modern Corporation and Private Property* (Harcourt, Brace and World, New York, 1932–1968).

Berman, Harold J., *Justice in the USSR* (Harvard University Press, Cambridge Mass., 1966).

Bettelheim, Charles, *Cultural Revolution and Industrial Organisation in China* (Monthly Review Press, New York, 1974).

Bottomore, Tom and Goode, Patrick, *Austro-Marxism* (Oxford University Press, 1978).

Bracher, Karl Dietrich, *The German Dictatorship* (Penguin Books, Harmondsworth, 1973).

Bukharin, Nikolai, *Imperialism and World Economy* (Merlin Books, London, 1972).

Bukharin, Nikolai, *Economics of the Transition Period* (Routledge and Kegan Paul, London, 1979).

Cutler, Antony, Hindess, Barry, Hirst, Paul, and Hussain, Athar, *Marx's Capital and Capitalism Today*, Vols 1 and 2 (Routledge and Kegan Paul, London, 1977–8).

Descartes, Rene, *Discourse on Method* (Penguin Books, 1960).

Diamond, Lord, *Royal Commission on the Distribution of Income and Wealth*, Report No. 2, Cmnd. 6172 (HMSO, London, 1975).

Drucker, Peter, *The Concept of the Corporation* (New English Library, London, 1965).

Edelman, Bernard, *Ownership of the Image* (Routledge and Kegan Paul, London, 1979).

Fishman, David, 'Analysis of the British Financial System'. Paper presented to CSE Money Group (Mimeo, 1976).

Formoy, R. R., *The Historical Foundations of Modern Company Law* (Sweet and Maxwell, London, 1923).

Freud, Sigmund, 'The Unconscious', *Standard Edition*, Vol. XIV (Hogarth Press, London, 1915).

Hacking, Ian, *Why Does Language Matter to Philosophy?* (Cambridge University Press, 1975).

Hadden, Tom, *Company Law and Capitalism* (Weidenfeld and Nicholson, London, 1st Edn. 1972, 2nd Edn. 1977).

Hall, Stewart, 'Some problems with the ideology/subject couplet', *Ideology and Consciousness*, No. 3 (Spring 1978).

Hilferding, Rudolf, *Le Capital Financier* (1910) (Minuit, Paris, 1970).

Hilferding, Rudolf, *Bohm-Bawerk's Criticism of Marx* (Merlin Press, London, 1975).

Hindess, Barry, 'Introduction' to C. Bettelheim, *Economic Calculation and Forms of Property* (Routledge and Kegan Paul, London, 1976).

Hindess, Barry, *Philosophy and Methodology in the Social Sciences* (Harvester Press, Hassocks, 1977).

Hindess, Barry & Hirst, Paul, *Pre-Capitalist Modes of Production* (Routledge and Kegan Paul, London, 1975).

Hindess, Barry & Hirst, Paul, *Mode of Production and Social Formation* (Macmillan, London, 1977).

Hirst, Paul, 'Marx and Engels on Law, Crime and Morality', *Economy and Society*, Vol. 1 No. 1 (1972).

Hirst, Paul, 'Economic Classes and Politics' in A. Hunt (ed) *Class and Class Structure* (Lawrence & Wishart, London, 1977).

Holloway, John and Picciotto, Sol (eds.), *State and Capital* (Edward Arnold, London, 1978).

Hope, 'On Being Taken Over by Slater-Walker', *The Journal of Industrial Economics*, Vol. XXIV, No. 3 (March 1976).

Hunt, Bishop Carleton, *The Development of the Business Corporation in England 1800–1867* (1936 – reprinted Russell and Russell, New York, 1969).

Hussain, Athar, 'Hilferding's *Finance Capital*', *Bulletin of the Conference of Socialist Economists* Vol. VI, No. 13 (1976).

Kelsen, Hans, *General Theory of Law and State* (1945 – reprinted Russell and Russell, New York, 1961).

Kelsen, Hans, *What is Justice?* (University of California Press, Los Angeles, 1971).

Kirchheimer, Otto, 'Criminal Law in National Socialist Germany', *Studies in Philosophy and Social Science* Vol. XIII, No. 3 (1940).

Kirchheimer, Otto, *Political Justice* (Princeton University Press, New Jersey, 1961).

Krausnik, Helmut and Broszat, Martin, *Anatomy of the SS State* (Paladin, St Albans, 1973).

Lacan, Jacques, 'The Mirror Phase', *New Left Review*, 51 (1968).

Lenin, V. I., *The State and Revolution, Collected Works*, Vol. 25 (Progress Publishers, Moscow, 1964).

Locke, John, *Two Treatises of Government* (New English Library, London, 1965).

Lukács, Georg, *History and Class Consciousness* (Merlin Press, London, 1971).

Marriot, Oliver, *The Property Boom* (Pan, London, 1969).

Marx, Karl, *Critique of Hegel's Philosophy of Right, Collected Works*, Vol. 3 (Lawrence & Wishart, London, 1975).

Marx, Karl, *1844 Manuscripts*, *CW*, Vol. 3 (1975).

Marx, Karl and Engels, Frederick, *The German Ideology CW*, Vol. 5 (1976).

Marx, Karl and Engels, Frederick, '1857 Introduction' and

'1859 Preface' to *A Contribution to the Critique of Political Economy* (Lawrence & Wishart, London, 1971).

Marx, Karl and Engels, Frederick, *Capital*, Vols. I and III (Progress Publishers, Moscow, 1965 and 1962).

Macpherson, C. B., *The Political Theory of Possessive individualism* (Oxford University Press, 1962).

McLennan, Gregor, 'On *Mode of Production and Social Formation*', *Economy and Society* Vol. 7, No. 2 (1978).

Miller, Jacques-Alain, 'On the Function of Theoretical Training', *Cahiers Marxiste-Leninistes*, No. 1, Translated in *Theoretical Practice*, No. 6, p. 49.

Neumann, Franz, *Behemoth* (1942 – Harper and Row, New York, 1966).

Pashukanis, E. B., *General Theory of Law and Marxism*, in Babb (1951) above. Also Ink Links (London, 1978).

Patrick, Hugh and Rosovsky, Henry (eds.), *Asia's New Giant* (The Brookings Institution, Washington, 1976).

Poulantzas, Nicos, *Fascism and Dictatorship* (New Left Books, London, 1974).

Rancière, Jacques, 'The concept of "Critique" and the "Critique of Political Economy"' in *Theoretical Practice*, Nos. 1, 2 and 6 (1971–72), and *Economy and Society*, Vol. 5, No. 3 (1976).

Renner, Karl, *The Institutions of Private Law and their Social Functions* (Introduction by O. Kahn-Freund) (Routledge and Kegan Paul, London, 1949 – reprinted 1976).

Rubin, I. I., *Essays on Marx's Theory of Value* (Black and Red, Detroit, 1972).

Rusche, G. and Kirchheimer, O., *Punishment and Social Structures* (1939 – reprinted Russell and Russell, New York, 1963).

Sharlet, Robert, 'Pashukanis and the Withering Away of Law in the USSR', in Sheila Fitzpatrick (ed.), *Cultural Revolution in Russia 1928–1931* (Indiana University Press, Bloomington, Ind., 1974).

Thompson, Grahame, 'The relationship between the financial and industrial sector in the UK economy', *Economy and Society*, Vol. 6, No. 3 (August 1977).

Thompson, Grahame, 'Some issues in the development of

accountancy'. Paper presented to CSE Money Group (Mimeo, 1976).

Wittkower, Rudolf, *Allegory and the Migration of Symbols* (Thames and Hudson, London, 1976).